How to Read
the Bible
So It Changes Your Life

Aletha Hinthorn

Beacon Hill Press of Kansas City
Kansas City, Missouri

Library of Congress Cataloging-in-Publication Data

Hinthorn, Aletha.
   How to read the Bible so it changes your life / Aletha Hinthorn.
      p. cm.
   Includes bibliographical references.
   ISBN 0-8341-2137-9 (pbk.)
   1. Bible—Reading. I. Title.

   BS617 .H53 2004
   220—dc22

2004015091

10 9 8 7 6 5 4 3 2 1

Contents

1

From "Ought" to Thirst

I HAVE NOT ALWAYS HAD A DEEP DESIRE TO READ SCRIPTURE. Our daughter Arla was a baby in the mid-70s, and nearly every morning after my husband, Daniel, had taken our son to school and gone on to work, I enjoyed a quiet hour alone. My habit was to read the newspaper and enjoy a leisurely cup of coffee before Arla awoke.

Seldom did I consider this to be a productive time, and one morning I sensed an emptiness, a hunger for more than I knew I would find in the *Kansas City Star*. I stepped over to our bookshelf and randomly pulled out a book. I opened it to these words: "God's Word can be as fresh to you as the daily newspaper."

Struck by this remarkable and possibly direct message, I knew it was up to me to rearrange the newspaper and the Bible on my priority list. I canceled the newspaper and began each morning sitting at my kitchen table with an open Bible and a cup of coffee.

A few months passed. One morning, eager to learn if a candidate for whom I had given a tea had won a local election, I rushed out to get the free weekly paper I knew the paperboy had thrown onto our lawn.

While walking back into the house, I thought, *I'll wait to read the newspaper and will have my cup of coffee with my Bible reading—because I'll enjoy reading that more than the newspa-*

per. I then realized that although reading the Word regularly had begun as a discipline, it had become my preferred pleasure.

Ben Patterson, a campus pastor, speaks in *Deepening Your Conversation with God* about his habit of rising early to be in solitude. He says that in all honesty he gets up not to achieve an elite level of spiritual athleticism; he gets up because it's so good and pleasant to do so. He can hardly call it a discipline anymore. "It is so delicious, so ineffably sweet, to hear the Lord, the Good Shepherd, speak or even to hope that He might," he says. It isn't so much that God speaks directly during those times; rather, the stillness prepares Patterson to be alert to those whispers and nudges he might receive as he drives his car or walks across campus.[1]

"Desire the pure milk of the word, that you may grow," (1 Pet. 2:2, NKJV) wrote Peter, implying that our spiritual maturity hinges on our acquiring this craving. So how do we gain a longing for spiritual food? Desire for Scripture begins with an act of the will. We choose to set aside time to read and meditate regularly. We begin doing what we *would* do *if* we had a consuming hunger to know Him better.

Strong desires begin as *small* desires, but how easy it is to quench small desires simply by ignoring the drawing of the Spirit! Desire cannot be forced, but even a little desire can be encouraged to grow stronger, like a spark fanned into full flame. Our first step is to tell God humbly and truthfully of our desire to have fellowship with Him. Then we follow the ideas He brings.

Phillip Henry, father of Matthew, who authored the Matthew Henry Commentaries, often said, "All grace grows as love to the word of God grows."[2] Our spiritual renewal depends upon our desire for the Word. The introduction to Ezra in the *Touchpoint Bible* puts it this way: "All great spiritual movements or revivals must be built on a love for God's Word, the Bible, and a passion to live it and talk about it."

Some years ago a friend said that she wanted to be with the

Lord and sense His presence, so she began taking her Bible with her to work and found time to be alone with God on her lunch hour. "I sensed that God was pleased with my efforts to commune with Him," she said. God notices our every expression of spiritual hunger no matter how small.

God Makes a Way

God is so eager to meet with us regularly that He ensures our ability to spend time with Him when we deliberately choose to listen to Him. He did this for Mary. He promised that her choice to sit at His feet "[would] not be taken away" (Luke 10:42).

When Mary sat at the feet of Jesus, I imagine she was getting plenty of silent looks from her sister, Martha, long before Martha said anything—looks that said, "You should be helping me!" If Mary had permitted her sister's disapproving gaze to cause her to feel guilty, she would have excused herself from Jesus' presence rather than yield to the desire in her heart. Once she had excused herself from sitting at His feet, her desire to listen eventually would have diminished.

But when she allowed herself to "waste" that time, Jesus defended her. "Choose to sit at My feet, and I will make a way. I will ensure your ability to spend time with Me. It's your choice."

Jesus still defends us when we choose to spend time at His feet. When we make listening to Him a priority, we find that He again says, "That time will not be taken away." He makes a way where there seems to be no way, in part by increasing our desire so that spending time with Him is no longer a mere discipline. In time, we find that meeting with Him is the "solid joy" of our day.

In his excellent devotional book *This Day with the Master,* Dennis Kinlaw tells of a choice he made that has made all the difference in his life.[3] When he was a freshman in college, he had a hunger to please God and to know Him better. Kinlaw knew a senior who exhibited remarkable maturity and decided to ask him how to grow more quickly in his Christian life. The friend asked Kinlaw how much time he spent alone with God. Kinlaw is sure he exaggerated the amount of time when he responded. The friend replied simply, "Double it." That ended their conversation.

His friend's pattern was to have quiet time first thing in the morning. Kinlaw had a bakery job that began quite early, and the prospect of following his friend's example was not an easy one. Still, he set his alarm clock for an earlier time and tried to do what his friend suggested.

Kinlaw states, "Only God knows how many times I fell asleep on my knees as I tried to begin my day with God." But he has no regrets about that, because a habit was being formed without which his life would have been tragically empty. Slowly, what he did in duty became a delight. He found he could live without other things, but he could not live without time with Christ.

Intimacy Is God's Idea

When we come to the Word with a consuming desire, it is for one reason—because God, who longs for this much more passionately than we do, has placed a hunger in our hearts. "Thirsty hearts are those whose longings have been wakened by the touch of God within them," wrote A. W. Tozer.

Intimacy was God's idea. He seeks our fellowship, and He has given us that desire. Hear the late Robb French's description of God's desire to have us near Him.

Adam and Eve had the privilege of walking with God in the cool of the day. That was wonderful. But God said, "I want to come closer than that."

God came down on Mt. Sinai and invited Moses to enter into His very presence. There in that awesome majesty, God revealed His law. That was wonderful. But God said, "I want to come closer than that. I want to enter into intimate fellowship with humanity."

So He commanded Moses to build a tabernacle. And in the tabernacle he placed the ark and the mercy seat. Then God came down. The Talmud claims that a pale blue light hovered over the mercy seat. God dwelt in the holy of holies in the tabernacle. But God said, "I want to come closer than that."

Again God came down. This time in the form of human flesh. He was born as a babe and dwelt among us. He suffered and died for us, and yet amazingly, God said, "I want to come closer than that."

"If you will tarry in the upper room, I will come down and move inside of you." That is almost too sacred to talk about! What wonder! The triune God, in the person of the Holy Ghost, dwelling in this unworthy temple of mine![4]

How does your heart respond when you read God's words in Jer. 30:21? "Who is he who will devote himself to be close to me?" questions the Lord.

If your heart's response is an eager "I will!" it is because God has placed His desire in your heart. Respond to that desire.

MEDITATION

Hear the breathless musings of the biblical writers as they think on God's Word. Consider how your life would be enriched by developing such cravings.

These Words Are Life

"My soul thirsts for you like a parched land" (Ps. 143:6).

"How sweet are your words to my taste; they are sweeter than honey" (Ps. 119:103, NLT).

"They are more desirable than gold, even the finest gold. They are sweeter than honey, even honey dripping from the comb" (Ps. 19:10, NLT).

"Your law is more valuable to me than millions in gold and silver!" (Ps. 119:72, NLT).

"I have treasured the words of his mouth more than my daily bread" (Job 23:12).

"When your words came, I ate them; they were my joy and my heart's delight" (Jer. 15:16).

"I rejoice in your word like one who finds a great treasure" (Ps. 119:162, NLT).

"Wisdom is more precious than rubies, and nothing you desire can compare with her" (Prov. 8:11).

What does the Spirit say to me through these words?

How will I respond?

"For he spoke"—that's my desire, Lord: to hear You speak. May this desire become a passion that orders my days.

2 There Is Power in the Word

ANN PRESTON, ALSO KNOWN AS HOLY ANN, was a simple Irish lady. Her education began and ended in little more than a week, but in that time she exhausted the patience of her teacher. After many vain attempts to teach her the first letters of the alphabet, her teacher gave her a tap upon the head as he pathetically remarked before the class, "Poor Ann! She can never learn anything!" With this she was sent home in disgrace.[1]

Years later, Ann became a Christian, and her first prayer was *O Lord, couldn't You enable me to read one of these things?* She put her finger on John 4:13-14 and began to read for the first time in her life: "Whosoever drinketh of this water shall thirst again: but whosoever drinketh of the water that I shall give him shall never thirst" (KJV). Eventually Ann could freely read the Word of God, although she could never read any other book.

The Bible is unlike any other book. "The Holy Spirit . . . imparted a power to the words which make them permanently living and effective," wrote W. E. Vine in *Divine Inspiration of the Bible.*[2] Again and again the Scriptures declare that these are supernatural words with life in them. "The words I have spoken to you are spirit and they are life" (John 6:63). "They are not just idle words for you—they are your life" (Deut. 32:47). "The Word that God speaks is alive and full of power" (Heb. 4:12, AMP.). The Greek word translated "full of power" means "power

11

in action." The Word, then, is not merely potential power. It is God's power in action. It is doing His work.[3]

The Word Is a Word

When Marvin Powers was serving in the army, he left the barracks one Sunday afternoon to sit under a tree and read his Bible. He noticed a man reading a book and felt compelled to go near him. As he got closer, he saw the insignia of the Chinese air force on his uniform and the name Shi-chi-kan. In trying to make conversation with him, Marvin soon discovered the man could not speak English, so they practiced pronouncing each other's names. Then Marvin tapped on his open Bible and pointed to the sky and then to his chest. The man watched intently, finally smiled, and walked off.

Marvin returned to the barracks and, out of concern for this new friend, contacted the American Bible Society to request a Chinese Bible. In a few days it arrived, and Marvin headed over to the Chinese barracks. He walked in and told the officer, "I'm looking for Shi-chi-kan."

The officer spoke English and told Marvin that Shi-chi-kan was in the next room. Marvin showed the officer the Book he had brought and asked him to find John, then chapter 3, and finally verse 16.

Marvin kept his finger on John 3:16 as he walked into the next room, and just as he had prayed, Shi-chi-kan was alone. "I have a book I want you to read," Marvin said, pointing to John 3:16. Shi-chi-kan began reading.

Finally, Shi-chi-kan closed the Book. Marvin tapped on the Bible, pointed to the sky, then to His chest and said, "We pray," and got on his knees. Shi-chi-kan knelt beside him. Marvin prayed in English. His friend said some Chinese words, and then he looked at Marvin with a big smile and pointed to the sky and then to his chest. They arose, and Shi-chi-kan continued smiling and laughing. He had received Jesus into His heart. Reading those few words of Scripture had activated his faith.

They soon parted, but Shi-chi-kan later wrote to Marvin. The letters contained few words Marvin could make out except "I love Jesus."

The gospel doesn't just tell about God's power. "The gospel . . . is the power of God" (Rom. 1:16). God's Word brings the presence and the power of God into our lives.

Hear the Word

Hearing about the Word does not change our lives, though. Hearing the Word itself brings about the changes. My brother Winston teaches a university class called "New Testament Survey," and he assures me that most of his students enroll because their degrees require his class rather than out of any desire to study Scripture.

In previous classes, he gave an overview of the Bible, but last semester he required that they read the Word. He gave his students a list titled "The Most Important Questions" and Bible references they were to study. His questions ranged from "Is it possible for one to know for certain that he or she will go to Heaven when he or she leaves this world?" (1 John 3:14-15; 2 Tim. 4:6-7; Acts 7:54-60) to "Why is 'Where will I spend eternity?' such an important question?" (Matt. 16:24-27; 2 Cor. 5:10; Rev. 20; 22:12-15; Matt. 25:41-46).

Winston read me some of the students' evaluations:

"This class has changed my life."

"God ordained this for this time in my life."

"This class has affected my life more than I can possibly imagine."

"This class has renewed my faith."

Students were beginning to attend church, and many had a renewed interest in God.

Wonderful books about the Bible, no matter how insightful

they may be, lack the power of the Word. Repeatedly, God tells us what His Word accomplishes. "By the word of the LORD were the heavens made, their starry host by the breath of his mouth" (Ps. 33:6). By the power of His spoken word, God willed creation into existence. He said, "Let there be light," and there was light. He sent forth His word, and the ice melted. He spoke a word, and people were healed. (Gen. 1:3; Ps. 33:6; 147:18; 107:20).

Hear and Obey

God works by speaking. Martin Luther said, "God's works are His words." We do our work simply by believing His Word. When the disciples asked Jesus, "What must we do to do the works God requires?" He told them simply to believe (John 6:28-29). It's fascinating that God's work and our work are both done through His Word. He speaks it, and we believe it.

The following incident, described by Edith Knipmeyer, a tiny lady who has since gone to heaven, reveals the power of the words the Spirit speaks to our spirits.

When I was reading your magazine, *Women Alive!* I noticed you were asking for answers to prayer. The Lord made it plain to me that I should write about one of my miraculous answers to prayer.

When we lived on the farm, my husband, Virgil, usually fattened several head of steers in the winter. One morning when Virgil left for work, he said, "Now when you call the trucker, tell him that if he thinks he'll get stuck not to come. There isn't enough power on the farm to pull the truck out.

The truck came, and we loaded those big steers. I believe there were at least 38 head. When they were loaded, the truck would not move. The wheels didn't even try to move.

I was standing in front of the truck. The Lord told me to go to the back and push. I never said anything, but I thought that sure would be foolish.

The men added a second tractor, but the truck still didn't move.

I went to the back and placed my hand on the truck but never pushed.

That act of obedience caused Edith to hear these words: "I will not fail thee now." Then she began pushing with all her might, and those big truck wheels slowly began to move!

What a true-to-life picture of God's response to our obedience! At times we may look at one of God's commands and think, *Impossible!* And God is probably saying, *Of course you can't, but I can! You push. You do your part. Act as though you can.*

It is in our willingness to respond to the Word that we discover its power. The Word of the Lord is the sword of the Spirit (see Eph. 6:17). A single phrase can melt, comfort, or transform us. We simply need to receive it and obey it.

MEDITATION

Consider the profound implications of the truths acknowledged in the following verses. How can we read His powerful life-giving Words and not bow in awe?

These Words Are Life

"They are not just idle words for you—they are your life" (Deut. 32:47).

"The Word that God speaks is alive and full of power" (Heb. 4:12, AMP.).

"The LORD merely spoke, and the heavens were created. He breathed the word, and all the stars were born" (Ps. 33:6, NLT).

"The Son is the radiance of God's glory and the exact representation of his being, sustaining all things by his powerful word" (Heb. 1:3).

"Above all, you must understand that no prophecy in Scripture ever came from the prophets themselves or because they wanted to prophesy. It was the Holy Spirit who moved the prophets to speak from God" (2 Pet. 1:20-21, NLT).

"The grass withers and the flowers fall, but the word of our God stands forever" (Isa. 40:8).

"My word that goes out from my mouth . . . will not return to me empty, but will accomplish what I desire and achieve the purpose for which I sent it" (Isa. 55:11).

"Heaven and earth will pass away, but my words will never pass away" (Matt. 24:35).

"The words I have spoken to you are spirit and they are life" (John 6:63).

What does the Spirit say to me through these words?

How will I respond?

Lord, I pray that through my obedience the power of Your Word becomes the power in my life.

3

Lord, Prepare
My Heart

MY FRIEND BECKY LOVES TO GARDEN. Early in the season she carefully places mulch around her plants so that they retain moisture. She ran short of mulch this year, and a few plants struggled through our hot, dry summer without the protective layer of mulch.

Becky noticed that the plants lacking mulch were not thriving. "I blasted them with water," she recalled, "but without mulch, the topsoil had hardened around the plants, so most of the water ran off. Being impatient, I didn't water long enough for the water to sink into the ground."

At times our Bible reading resembles Becky's watering of those unmulched plants. We go through the motions of feeding our spirits with truth. We hurriedly skim some verses without taking time for the Word to saturate our prepared hearts. Consequently, the truth runs off, and our spirits shrivel.

"The seed is the word of God" (Luke 8:11). What happens to the seed depends upon the state of the soil into which the seed falls. Seeds falling onto untended ground simply take no root and don't grow. God's seed is the Word, and if we're eager for His seed to take root in us, we'll want to prepare the ground of our hearts.

Hunger to Obey

"The essential condition of profitable Bible reading is not extensive learning or powerful intellect . . . but rather this, which is within the power of all of us—the honest desire to do God's will when we know it," states J. Paterson Smyth.[1]

At the close of one of my first days teaching at the Kansas School for the Blind, a fellow music teacher stood at the door of my studio and said, "You seem to be having a better start to your teaching than I did."

Tell her you prayed about it, the Spirit whispered.

Oh, but I don't know her well enough, I thought, dismissing the idea.

Later, I realized that failing to respond to the Spirit was a habit with me. I wanted with all my heart to do God's will, yet I frequently ignored His promptings.

One night in tears I laid my failures before the Lord. How could I ever change? The Spirit gently spoke these words to my spirit: *You need to learn to obey Me.*

I arose from prayer with a new resolution. I began coming to Scripture with a new heart hunger. The next morning I approached the Word differently—eager to obey the words I read. No longer was reading routine. No longer was I simply curious about what Scripture says; I hungered for the words to become part of my very being.

John Wesley said we are to read the Word with "a fixed resolution to do it." This resolve became the key to my new approach to Scripture. I had an inner hunger at the center of my being to obey whatever I found in the Word. How could I apply this verse? What did this passage say about my actions or attitudes?

The Holy Spirit faithfully showed me, but He did more than just point to needed changes. I discovered that when I did something in response to scripture, I was enabled to do what I needed to do. The Word has power, and to put it into my life was to add power.

More important than what we read or how we study is the attitude we bring to it. It's possible to be content with intriguing insights and enjoy thinking about passing them on to others, but if we do that, we miss the joy! If we seek to make our lives an expression of the Word's truth, we'll experience His blessing. Happy are those who hear the word of God and keep it!

Acknowledge the Teacher

The Holy Spirit wants to teach all who are eager to obey, just as Jesus taught His disciples when He was here. "Then he opened their minds so they could understand the Scriptures" (Luke 24:45). He invites us to begin reading with a conscious dependence upon the Spirit to teach us to listen and to be our Guide.

"God has actually given us his Spirit . . . so we can know the wonderful things God has freely given us" (1 Cor. 2:12, NLT). The Spirit reveals to us what God is thinking! Our own intellects reveal only what is humanly possible to understand, but we're looking for those truths the Spirit wants to reveal.

The Spirit wants us to acknowledge God's presence with us here and now. We may or may not sense His presence, but we can affirm through faith that the Holy One is attending to us. He is fully present. George Fox said, "It is a wonderful discovery to find that you are a temple, that you have a church inside of you, where God is. In hushed silence, attend to him. The Lord is in his holy temple."[2]

Many times we have no conscious sense of His presence, but we are to trust that the Spirit indwells us to teach us. When we treat Him as if He were in us (and He is) and we in Him, He will respond to our trust. The consciousness of His presence will become real and delightful.

How long we pray before we begin reading the Word is not nearly so important as our hunger to receive a fresh word, our daily manna. Sometimes we pray a prayer such as Samuel's

"Speak, Lord, for your servant is listening" (1 Sam. 3:9). Or we use David's words "Open my eyes that I may see wonderful things in your law" (Ps. 119:18). When we hunger and thirst and express sincere desire for the Spirit to teach us, we're opening ourselves to receive true riches that only the Spirit can give.

Before we begin eating, we ask God to bless the food to the use of our body. Isn't it equally fitting to ask Him to bless His Word to the use of our spirits before we begin reading? When we come to a difficult passage in our Bible reading, instead of giving up or rushing to a commentary, we should lay that passage before God and ask Him to explain it, remembering His promise "If any of you lacks wisdom, he should ask God" (James 1:5).

This request for understanding pleases God. When God offered Solomon his choice of all gifts, Solomon asked for understanding. God was so pleased that He gave him wealth, riches, and honor also (see 2 Chron. 1:12).

Andrew Murray, a brilliant writer on prayer, gave these weighty words on Bible reading: "Meditate a moment in silence on the thought that the words come from God Himself. Bow in deep reverence. Be silent unto God. Let Him reveal His Word in your heart. . . . As you read, remember that God's Word and God's Spirit are inseparable."[3]

Be a Receiver

The Bible differs from the Koran and all other religious books in that the Author of Scripture promises to teach us as we read. When the Holy Spirit enters our spirits, He enables us to comprehend His Word. I was happy to discover that the Lord asks us to be receivers of His truth rather than brilliant enough to discover its meaning on our own. To those who say, "But I can't get anything out of the Bible when I read it by myself," He replies, *Allow Me to teach you. Be a receiver.*

"The LORD gives wisdom" (Prov. 2:6); we're not dependent upon our own intellects. God doesn't say, "Figure this out on your own" but "Think about what I am saying. The Lord will give you understanding in all these things" (2 Tim. 2:7, NLT). This verse encourages us when we feel too dense to benefit from the Word. We're merely the ones who consider. Ask, seek, and knock, and the truth will be opened to you—we don't open it ourselves. Our role is simply to watch and listen daily at Wisdom's gate (Prov. 8:34-35). If we do, the promise is definite: He who seeks finds (Matt. 7:8).

Whenever truth comes, it's not because we're clever; it's because we've opened our minds to the Holy Spirit, and He has revealed truth to us. Our role is to be eager listeners, ones who are attentive with deep spiritual hunger. God interprets our efforts to gain understanding as desire for Him and promises, "Those who seek me [wisdom] find me" (Prov. 8:17).

Two lovers don't spend time with one another just so they can fill a notebook with insights or so they can tell someone else what they've learned. They just want to know the one they love. That longing is what Paul was describing when he said, "That I may know him" (Phil. 3:10, KJV). When a yearning to know Him—when desire to please Him—is at the center of our being, He reveals himself to us.

MEDITATION

God meets us in His Word when He sees our hearts call out, "I long to obey your commandments!" (Ps. 119:40, NLT). Reflect on these verses, and find one that resonates with your spirit. Allow these words to give you assurance that God will speak personally to you when you read scripture.

These Words Are Life

"Blessed are you . . . for this was not revealed to you by man, but by my Father in heaven" (Matt. 16:17).

"Then he opened their minds so they could understand the Scriptures" (Luke 24:45).

"God has actually given us his Spirit . . . so we can know the wonderful things God has freely given us" (1 Cor. 2:12, NLT).

"If any of you lack wisdom, let him ask of God" (James 1:5, KJV).

"The LORD gives wisdom" (Prov. 2:6).

"Reflect on what I am saying, for the Lord will give you insight into all this" (2 Tim. 2:7).

"Were not our hearts burning within us while he talked with us on the road and opened the Scriptures to us?" (Luke 24:32).

What does the Spirit say to me through these words?

How will I respond?

Lord, I come to the Word for this purpose—to hear what the Spirit wants to say to me. Give me a listening heart.

4

Listening with All Our Hearts

I RECENTLY SAW BOOKS IN A LOCAL BOOKSTORE TITLED *How to Learn the Bible in 24 Hours* and *Find It Fast in the Bible*. In fact, my mission was to purchase *Getting Things Done*, a book someone had told me would help me write this book more quickly.

Such books appeal to those of us who are becoming what Sue Monk Kidd calls "quickaholics." If we can get our glasses made in one hour and our oil changed in ten minutes, why shouldn't we be able to accelerate our time alone with God?

Years ago our family received a flyer for a book titled *How to Have Devotions in Five Minutes*, and our son commented, "We should get that for Grandma. It would save her so much time." My mother's approach to the Word was much like that of the Scripture writers. They thought about the words, pondered them, and listened attentively because they intended to take them to heart.

Jesus frequently said, "Anyone who is willing to hear should listen and understand!" (Matt. 13:9, NLT). He wanted His listeners to do more than repeat to Him what He had said. He wanted His words to sink into their spirits and to be expressed through their lives.

Sometimes our comprehension of what we've read is remarkably similar to that of five-year-old Garrett, who was eager to show his dad, Andy Stanley, what he could read. They sat down on the floor together, and Garrett began:

"A man gave an old coat to an old goat. That old goat said, 'I will eat this old coat.' So he did. 'That was fun,' he said. 'I ate the old coat, and now I am cold.' And now the old goat is sad."

It took Garrett about three minutes to get through those lines. When he finished, his dad asked him a few questions to test his comprehension.

"Garrett, what did the old man give to the goat?"

"What man?"

"The man in the story. The man in the story gave something to an old goat. What did he give him?"

"I don't know."

"He gave him a coat. The old man gave the goat a coat. What did the goat do with the coat?"

"Wear it?"

"No, he ate it."

"That's funny, Daddy."

It was evident that Garrett and his daddy had two different agendas. Garrett just wanted to sound out the words correctly. His dad wanted him to read and comprehend.[1]

What is our agenda when we come to the Word of God? We come not only to comprehend but also to be changed. God told the prophet Ezekiel, "'Son of man, eat what I am giving you— eat this scroll!' . . . So I opened my mouth, and he fed me the scroll." [Notice that all Ezekiel had to do was open his mouth. He was merely a receiver.]

"'Eat it all,' he said. And when I ate it, it tasted as sweet as honey.

"Then he said, 'Son of man, go to the people of Israel with my message'" (Ezek. 3:1-4, NLT).

God wanted Ezekiel to digest the Word and turn it into his own flesh so people would see the Word of God in a living body rather than on a dead parchment. This is the change that occurs when we receive the Word into our lives. People once again see the Word become flesh.

What Jesus wants is not simple imitation. (As Ronald Rolheiser says, no one does Jesus very well anyway!)[2] Rather, Jesus wants to live through us as we receive His Word, His life. Then we become the Living Word.

With His words in our spirits, we have His life. Without them, our spirits are dead, empty, lifeless. We realize the truth that Jesus taught: without His words, "you have no life in you" (John 6:53).

The Art of Listening

When we read in order to become living epistles, we're reading not simply for information—we're reading for personal transformation. We come to the Word not simply to learn what it says but to allow it to shape us, to form our thinking. One sentence may be all we read, but we dwell on it.

The Word transforms us when we expect to encounter God and to be changed. We come humbly, ready to do what He says. We don't read merely to "have devotions" but to respond in love to whatever God desires.

Compare the way we read a letter from a close friend to the way we skim the newspaper for news. Reading that invites the life of God into our spirits has more in common with reading a letter from a friend. We read as though we're savoring the words of a love letter or pondering the meaning of a poem. We aren't skimming over the surface of an article in a popular magazine. Instead, we're reading and rereading scripture and listening for the words that resonate.

Listening with all our hearts entails reading each sentence as if for the first time, expecting God to give us a personal message. Once we've read a thought that seems meant for us, we start dwelling on it. We may want to stay in a "holding pattern" over a single phrase or verse and ask, *God, what are You saying to me just now?* To listen with our hearts, we must engage our minds.

When God gave us the ability to imagine, He expected us to use it in our relationships with Him. He's pleased when we read His Words and allow our imaginations to help us see beyond what the words say. If the passage is a narrative with characters, it may help to imagine the setting of the story and to envision ourselves in it. Who can we identify with? For instance, if we read about Mary Magdalene washing Jesus' feet, we might ask ourselves, *How would I feel if I were expressing my love to Jesus by washing His feet? How can I experience that same passionate devotion? Would I have been willing to kneel at His feet while those nearby were scoffing?*

Madame Guyon wrote, "If you read quickly, it will benefit you little. You will be like a bee that merely skims the surface of a flower. Instead, in this new way of reading with prayer, you must become as the bee who penetrates into the depths of the flower. You plunge deeply within to remove its deepest nectar."[3]

Dallas Willard compares our carefully observing the Word with smelling the roses. "To enjoy the rose it is necessary to focus on it and bring the rose as fully before our senses and mind as possible. To smell a rose, you must get close and you must linger. When we do so, we delight in it. We love it."[4]

We read slowly in order to sense the heart of what God is saying. We declare with the psalmist, "I will listen to what God the LORD will say" (Ps. 85:8).

In his *Preface to Sermons*, John Wesley described his Bible reading: "Here then I am, far from the busy ways of men. I sit down alone: only God is here. In his presence I open, I read his Book; for this end, to find the way to Heaven." Remembering that God is here when we read His Word and that we are in His presence is the secret to listening with all our hearts.

Lessons from Two Listeners

In her autobiography *Hearing Heart*, Hannah Hurnard tells how she engaged her mind while listening with her heart. "He used my ordinary mental faculties and encouraged me to ask questions all the time. There was . . . no waiting for thoughts to come to me out of the blue. But he seemed to clarify my thoughts as I expressed my questions in words or in writing, and enabled me to think the answers he wanted me to receive."

Hannah said that often it was just her own thoughts that came to her as she pondered the subject, but she quickly became able to recognize the Lord's answers to her questions. His thoughts came with a clarity and a kind of illumination that her own conclusions lacked. It was as though all of a sudden something clicked in her mind. "Ah, that's it; that is what he wants me to understand. That's what he wants me to do. So that is the meaning of this passage; why did I never see it before?"[5]

Although we are not concerned with speed or volume read, reading that transforms our lives involves both time and intensity. Dallas Willard recalls the first time he spent the better part of a day just reading and rereading the Gospel of John. He was in his second year of college on a holiday weekend, which meant that the campus was largely deserted. He began by reading the Gospel while doing laundry. That was done in an hour or two, and by then he was engrossed in John's account.

"I did nothing for the rest of the day but live there in that world: reading, meditating, cross-referencing, and rereading. Truthfully, my world never looked quite the same after that day." He had discovered a reality in Jesus that he had never known before.

Willard says he learned through this experience that intensity is crucial in our attempts to gain spiritual understanding. "To dribble a few verses or chapters of Scripture on oneself through the week, in church or out, will not reorder one's mind and spirit—just as one drop of water every five minutes will not get you a shower, no matter how long you keep it up. You need a lot of water at once and for a sufficiently long time. Similarly for the written Word."[6]

We can come to this written Word forgetting that Christ desires to speak to us. When we listen intently, however, we'll hear His invitation to become the embodiment of the Word as He was. What an invitation!

Reading Meditatively

When we come to familiar scriptures, we may be tempted to say, "I've read that a dozen times. I could almost quote these verses. What can I possibly see new in it today?" Yet when we dwell upon the words, something fresh often comes. As a result, our spiritual lives may be deepened either by an old truth or by a new one.

For instance, let's reflect on the parable Jesus told of the woman who lost her coins:

"Suppose a woman has ten silver coins and loses one. Does she not light a lamp, sweep the house and search carefully until she finds it? And when she finds it, she calls her friends and neighbors together and says, 'Rejoice with me; I have found my lost coin'" (Luke 15:8-9).

I love her eagerness. It's the intense zeal Solomon envisioned when he told us how to gain insight and understanding. "Look for it as for silver and search for it as for hidden treasure" (Prov. 2:4). What a difference it makes when we begin as this lady did—certain that there's something valuable to find, and committed to searching until we find it!

The woman who lost the coins lights a lamp, reminding us that we cannot find truth in the Word without the spiritual illumination of the Holy Spirit. We earnestly pray, *Please, Lord— may the light of the Holy Spirit show me the treasure You have for me today.*

With her lamp lit, she begins to search eagerly and carefully for the valuable coin. We, too, must "sweep the words" with eagerness and great care, longing to glimpse a truth that will satisfy our spirits. With the Spirit's light, we examine every sentence and every word, turning them over in our minds, looking at them from different viewpoints. We ponder ways to apply the words in an effort to find some truth that will deepen our love and understanding of God.

Imagine the woman's excitement the moment her eyes lay hold on the silver coin. She no doubt values it even more because she had to search so diligently for it.

When we search for wisdom as though it were hidden treasure, we know the pleasure of discovering a gem of truth. Whether the passage has yielded a new thought or caused an old one to come alive once again, our spirits are satisfied.

"How sweet are your words to my taste, sweeter than honey to my mouth!" (Ps. 119:103).

MEDITATION

The Spirit looks for those who are eager to hear His voice. The word in Scripture translated "hear" or "listen" means to hear intelligently and to obey. Reflect on the following verses, and consider the importance of choosing to listen.

These Words Are Life

"Speak, LORD, for your servant is listening" (1 Sam. 3:9).

"Tune your ears to wisdom, and concentrate on understanding. Cry out for insight and understanding" (Prov. 2:2-3, NLT).

"Pay attention to what I say; listen closely to my words . . . for they are life to those who find them" (Prov. 4:20, 22).

"Anyone who is willing to hear should listen and understand!" (Matt. 13:9, NLT).

"If you look for me in earnest, you will find me when you seek me" (Jer. 29:13, NLT).

"I will listen to what God the LORD will say" (Ps. 85:8).

"Do not merely listen to the word, and so deceive yourselves. Do what it says" (James 1:22).

"Whoever has my commands and obeys them, he is the one

who loves me. He who loves me will be loved by my Father, and I too will love him and show myself to him" (John 14:21).

"Blessed are all who hear the word of God and put it into practice" (Luke 11:28, NLT).

"They made their hearts as hard as stone, so they could not hear the law or the messages that the LORD Almighty had sent them by his Spirit" (Zech. 7:12, NLT).

What does the Spirit say to me through these words?

How will I respond?

Dear Lord, I set my mind to gain understanding. I hunger to receive what You have for me this day.

5 Record the Treasures

"WISE MEN LAY UP KNOWLEDGE" (Prov. 10:14, KJV).

I love the lines Lewis Carroll wrote in *Alice in Wonderland*:

"'The horror of that moment,' the King went on, 'I shall never, never forget!'

'You will, though,' the Queen said, 'if you don't make a memorandum of it.'"

That's true, because, as someone has quipped, "The stubbiest pencil has a better memory than the most brilliant mind." I've thought, *I'll never forget this great idea!* and the next day—or even five minutes later—it will have completely evaporated from my mind and be gone forever.

One rainy Halloween our candy-loving daughter eagerly set out trick-or-treating with a paper bag. Not until she got home did she realize that her soggy bag was dispensing candy about as quickly as she dropped it in. Twenty years later she still recalls her disappointment. Often we collect treasures of truth in much the same way. We read the Word, and the Holy Spirit gives us a sweet nugget. We receive it eagerly and then put it in a bag with holes—our memories. Instead, we could place this truth in a safe place where the treasure will remain.

One of the ways I say, *Lord, I'm expecting to receive something too good to forget; I want to demonstrate my love for You by caring for wisdom when it comes* is to keep a notebook and pen handy while I read my Bible. Our treasures are the truths taught us by the Holy Spirit, and if we're wise, we'll carefully protect them.

When the burning bush appeared to Moses, he did a significant thing—he "turned aside to see" (Exod. 3:4, KJV). The way I "turn aside to see" is to write down a phrase or a verse that I would like to better understand or that I would like to live out in my life. If I sit down to read the Bible without my notebook, I feel as though I'm not really expecting to hear from the Lord. The notebook helps me to anticipate hearing my Father speak.

When David was giving his son Solomon the instructions for the Temple he was to build, David said, "All this . . . the LORD made me understand in writing by his hand upon me" (1 Chron. 28:19, KJV). While David wrote, the Lord gave him understanding. I've discovered that new insights often come while I write down a verse, perhaps because writing slows me down so I can consider carefully each detail. Recording what I'm reading becomes my way of saying to God, *Teach me what I should hear You say through this verse today.* He responds to this desire.

When we state in our own words what the Scripture says, we often begin longing more deeply for understanding. This happened to Zechariah. An angel awakened him and asked him what he saw. After describing the lamp stand and olive trees, Zechariah inquired, "What are these, my lord?" (Zech. 4:4).

God instructed the king to do more than simply read the Law: "When he takes the throne of his kingdom, he is to write for himself on a scroll a copy of this law" (Deut. 17:18). The process of writing truth would be more profitable to the king than merely reading it, just as it is for us.

The simple process of recording what I've read also makes me more likely to recall those words. One study showed that when we make the transition from passive listener to active listener by writing down what we've learned, our retention increases from 10 percent to 40 percent.

Treasure the Words

Wisdom calls out, "I love those who love me" (Prov. 8:17), and sends us ideas. If we love them, welcome and embrace them, wisdom will send us more. If we allow them to float away, like bubbles a child blows, their source will dry up. We show our appreciation for wisdom by recording it, placing it in a safe place.

The old-timers had a saying—"Fear [be in awe of] the passing of Jesus." The Living Word passes by, giving us glimpses of truth, fresh insights. We can allow these to be fleeting, or we can latch on to the truth, write it down, and make it a part of our thinking and living. "Wise men lay up knowledge" (Prov. 10:14, KJV). When we "fear the passing of truth," we invest in notebooks to store our treasures. These notebooks filled with reflections of Christ become more priceless than a family photo album.

Failing to record insights but going away and forgetting them is behaving like the man who finds a pearl, admires it, tosses it down, and continues on his way. Our insights are like found jewels. Are we going to pick them up, admire them, then toss them down, or are we going to place them in a treasure chest so we can go back later and admire them?

God intends for us to guard His teachings in the same way He guards His people. He keeps those He loves "as the apple of his eye" (Deut. 32:10, KJV). In Proverbs we're instructed, "Guard my teachings as the apple of your eye" (7:2).

The apple is the pupil or the center of the eye. In some versions the phrase "the apple of your eye" is translated "most precious possession." While it warms our hearts to think of God guarding us carefully, we can remember that He has asked us to value and give careful consideration to His teachings. Moses called the law "the special possession of the assembly of Israel" (Duet. 33:4, NLT). God asks us to keep His law as carefully as He keeps us.

"Every teacher of the law who has been instructed about the kingdom of heaven is like the owner of a house who brings out of his storeroom new treasures as well as old" (Matt. 13:52). I have a stack of storerooms—notebooks—that contain the insights I've collected over years of Bible reading. Matthew tells us that we'll have some old treasures, insights God gave us long ago that we loved enough to record, and new treasures, those fresh insights we gleaned in our more recent reading. The teacher of the law needs both.

Amy Carmichael, devotional writer and missionary to India during the first half of the 20th century, believed we should share insights. In *Whispers of His Power*, she commented on Prov. 12:27: "'The slothful man roasteth not that which he took in hunting: but the substance of a diligent man is precious.' What we learn is meant to be given to others. What are we doing with what we find in our Bibles? It must not be left like the talent in the napkin to do nothing for anyone."[1]

Maybe you think, *My ideas aren't worth recording*, but if we're faithful to record even those one-cent ideas, He will trust us with deeper truths. Jesus' words apply: "Whoever can be trusted with very little can also be trusted with much" (Luke 16:10).

Nineteenth-century Holiness theologian Phoebe Palmer stated that keeping a journal was so important that not to keep one is "almost a sin." She used her journal to record insights from the Scripture as well as to keep a record of God's dealing.[2]

Use your notebook-storehouse to record insights or reflections that have emerged in your reading and writing. Is there a verse that you would like to make yours by memorizing? Does the Spirit give you thoughts that stretch, deepen, or challenge you? Write how you hope to implement your "finds" in that day's reading.

Your "storehouse" can be a spiral notebook, a looseleaf notebook, or a plush journal. I like to stock up on spiral notebooks in August during the back-to-school sales. If my notebook costs only forty-nine cents, I can "waste" as many pages as I want by ignoring the voice that says, *That idea isn't worth recording*. Often a thought seems to have more value when reread weeks later. If only we could begin to realize the inestimable value of the insights the Holy Spirit desires to share with us, we would be as eager for truth as we are for gold and would keep it where we could find it later.

You may find it helpful to do other spiritual writing in your notebook. When you're facing doubts, try writing your thoughts to God. Once when I had grown weary of the doubts that had pursued me for days, I began to write, focusing on God and not on my doubts. My doubts lifted as I wrote scriptures and prayers. David often began his psalms writing notes of despair, but he encouraged himself in the Lord as he wrote, and his psalms often ended on a victorious note.

If you take seriously these suggestions to have a notebook and pen beside your Bible as you read, you'll someday look back and read today's treasure and think, *I had totally forgotten that insight.* It will mean even more on further reflection. That has happened to me repeatedly. I've come to acknowledge that when God makes a verse come alive in my spirit, He intends for me to dwell on the promise of those words again and again. Some of my most precious times in the Word occur as I reread journals filled with verses recorded long ago—verses I thought I would never forget. Fortunately, I had written them down.

MEDITATION

Don't you love to have someone think what you say is so important that he or she writes down your words? God is no less pleased when He sees you recording His wonderful truths. He knows you love His Word.

These Words Are Life

"Guard my teachings as the apple of your eye" (Prov. 7:2).

"My child, listen to me and treasure my instructions" (Prov. 2:1, NLT).

"Wise men store up knowledge" (Prov. 10:14).

"Write them on the doorposts of your house and on your gates" (Deut. 6:9, NLT).

"When he sits on the throne as king, he must copy these laws on a scroll for himself in the presence of the Levitical priests" (Deut. 17:18, NLT).

"Every teacher of the law who has been instructed about the kingdom of heaven is like the owner of a house who brings out of his storeroom new treasures as well as old" (Matt. 13:52).

"Write in a book all the words I have spoken to you" (Jer. 30:2).

"I will write down all these things as a testimony of what the LORD will do. I will entrust it to my disciples, who will pass it down to future generations" (Isa. 8:16, NLT).

What does the Spirit say to me through these words?

How will I respond?

I love the thoughts that come as I read Your Word, Lord. I write them down because I treasure them.

6 The Blessing of Listening Daily

"I CAN READ MY BIBLE REGULARLY for a couple weeks and then lose interest," a friend admitted. We can be all enthusiastic about being disciplined Bible readers, but there tends to be a short honeymoon with devotions. As Susan Muto observed, "The excitement of newness lasts for only a short while. It is then that we must apply the principle of 'stick-to-it-iveness.'"[1]

God told the Israelites to make their sacrifices regularly before the Lord, and then He promised, "I will meet you and speak to you" (Exod. 29:42). If their sacrifices had been hit or miss, they would have missed God's promise to reward their consistency by speaking to them. Only by meeting Him regularly can we learn to hear His voice.

When we begin to allow our daily time with God to slip away, we begin to miss it less and less. In an old journal I found this entry: "I awoke and realized that because I had not been reading [the Bible] consistently, my delight and excitement with God's Word wasn't as intense. This worries me." Our desire for the Word diminishes with neglect.

The result is that when a crisis comes, we discover we have little strength. We lack a vision of a God who is in control and "sits enthroned over the flood" (Ps. 29:10). Rather than seeing the Lord ruling the uncontrollable flood of problems in our lives, we simply see the flood and are overwhelmed. Only those who hold tightly to their time with God can confidently and calmly say, "All things serve you" (Ps. 119:91).

A lady who frequently speaks at women's retreats told me that God once gave her these instructions: *Less of your words; more of Mine.* She took that message to heart. She arises early each morning to meet with the Lord through His Word. She wrote the following E-mail after discovering a growth on her daughter's head where a malignancy had been removed. Her response reveals the confidence in God—a direct result of her time in God's Word:

> We must keep our focus by remembering that the Lord is in control. The first time her tumor appeared about two years ago, the Lord gave us a Scripture from Isaiah: "You will keep him in perfect peace, Whose mind is stayed on You, Because he trusts in You" (Isa. 26:3, NKJV). Isaiah . . . sang a song urging the Israelites . . . to keep their minds steady on God, who never loses control over events.

This mother's peace in the midst of overwhelming circumstances can be explained by her daily time of listening to the Word.

Planning to Listen

Just as God gave the Israelites fresh manna each day, He wants to give us something fresh from the Word each day. We become spiritually weak when we try to live for several days on what He's provided for today. We might think it makes little difference if we're not in the Word daily, but Solomon indicated that failing to listen regularly results in our wandering from the truth: "Stop listening to instruction, my son, and you will stray from the words of knowledge" (Prov. 19:27). Our ability to live by the Word hinges on our continually listening.

God implies that to forget Him is stranger than for a bride to forget her wedding ornaments: "Does a maiden forget her jewelry, a bride her wedding ornaments? Yet my people have forgotten me, days without number" (Jer. 2:32). With His Word being so crucial to our lives, why might we neglect it?

One of the reasons we fail to read God's Word regularly is that we don't plan to. We get up day after day, and we haven't decided what passage to read. Pressing duties soon sidetrack us, and another day passes without significant time with an open Bible. If we want renewal in our devotional lives badly enough, we'll make sufficient plans.

William Law's pointed words are helpful: "If you will here stop and ask yourself why you are not as pious as the primitive Christians were, your own heart will tell you that it is neither through ignorance nor inability, but purely because you never thoroughly intended it."

Zacchaeus "thoroughly intended" to see Jesus, so he planned ahead when Jesus was coming to his town. Being a "wee little man," "He ran before, and climbed up into a sycamore tree to see him" (Luke 19:3, KJV). He could have had plenty of excuses—"There are too many people." "I'm too short"—but what a rich blessing he would have missed!

Zacchaeus's planning paid off. Jesus looked up into that tree and called, "Zacchaeus, quick, come down! I must be a guest in your home today." Jesus notices when we plan our days around "seeing" Him. Often we find that the more regularly we arrange our day around seeing Him, the more we get done. Instead of crowding our day, it seems to ease the congestion!

For years I kept a handwritten note above my desk that challenged me to "Have done with lesser things." At times we need God to help us to both identify and eliminate those "lesser things," and we just forget to ask. A young man told me "I'll read for a couple days and then get busy, so one of my basic prayers is *God, give me the will to read.*"

One fellow said, "I used to write on my daily calendar, '7-7:30 A.M.—Prayer.' But many times I passed that up. It was one more thing to pass by that day. Now I write '7-7:30—God.' Somehow that's a little harder to neglect."

Yet He loves Us

Could God be saying, *I want to fill your life with spiritual blessing by speaking to you while you read My Word, but you won't give Me time to do anything for you?* With God's strength we can overcome the laziness that impoverishes our lives and say with King David, "God forbid that I should give to the Lord that which costs me nothing" (see 1 Chron. 21:24). Time in the Word often costs us effort, time, even sleep, but what a privilege it is to give Jesus something costly!

Denial may mean denying ourselves listening to the news while we drive to work so we can meditate on a verse we read that morning. It may mean denying ourselves an extra hour's sleep simply out of a desire to draw near. Some day it won't matter if we've been sleep-deprived, but we'll have all eternity to regret being God-deprived.

"A faithful man who can find?" (Prov. 20:6). Faithfulness is rare, but when God finds a faithful person, He takes special notice just as He did with Cornelius. Cornelius faithfully met with God, but surely there were days when he didn't feel like meeting his routine or didn't know if being devout made a difference. One day God sent an angel to tell him that his prayers "have come up as a memorial offering before God" (Acts 10:1-4). Our devotional habits tell God how strong our desires are to hear from Him, and He notices.

Setting aside our own agendas to meditate on the Word, whether we're fasting sleep, food, or favorite pastime, is an excellent way to draw near the Lord. Then we find that He draws near to us, and we say, *Better is one hour in Your presence than a thousand elsewhere.* We may make many choices for which we will one day be eternally grateful, but none more so than the choice to make sitting at Jesus' feet the most consistent part of our daily routines.

One morning nearly two decades ago I awakened early and sensed that the Holy Spirit was inviting me to get up and fellowship with Him. I almost got out of bed, but then I thought, "No, I'll sleep just a few more minutes." The next thing I knew the alarm was ringing, and another busy day was ahead with little time for private time with the Lord. The next morning, and for many mornings after that, there was no inner nudge to arise early.

I later wondered what my devotional life would have been like and what He might have taught me if I had responded to that gentle invitation. Yet our Father asks us to never doubt His love. He loves us when we spend time regularly with Him and when we don't.

Frances, a single friend of mine in Hawaii, is busy with work, ministry, and being a grandmother. She recently E-mailed me, "The last few weeks have been busy, and I have not been able to spend the quality time with Him that I desire. I miss it. I just watch God say, *It's OK,* by the little blessings He has bestowed on me. To me, that's His way of saying, *I'm still with you, and I know your concern.*"

Lord, increase my hunger to come to You regularly, and help me not doubt Your love when I've failed.

MEDITATION

Is God offering you an invitation to listen daily by bringing to your mind a time you could devote to Bible reading? If so, will you respond with anticipation and joyful obedience?

These Words Are Life

"When he sits on the throne as king, he . . . must always keep this copy of the law with him and read it daily as long as he lives. That way he will learn to fear the LORD his God by obeying all the terms of this law" (Deut. 17:18-19, NLT).

"Happy are those who listen to me, watching for me daily at my gates" (Prov. 8:34, NLT).

"Stop listening to instruction, my son, and you will stray from the words of knowledge" (Prov. 19:27).

"A faithful man who can find?" (Prov. 20:6).

"Better is one day in your courts than a thousand elsewhere" (Ps. 84:10).

"I listen carefully to what God the LORD is saying, for he speaks peace to his people" (Ps. 85:7, NLT).

What does the Spirit say to me through these words?

How will I respond?

Lord, I know You interpret my faithfulness as strong desire for Your Word. Place within my mind Your plan for my devotional life.

7 Beyond Memorizing

ONE EVENING WHILE PRAYING ABOUT A CONCERN I had repeatedly brought to the Lord, I wondered why I struggled to trust God. I prayed, *Dear Lord, You promised that if I am in You and You are in me, I could ask whatever I wanted and You would answer—so why am I struggling to believe?*

I hardly expected an answer, but soon after this prayer, the inner voice I have come to recognize said, *Praise God, because I want to hear you praise Me.*

Praising God because I knew He desired it was a joyful thing to do. The next morning I read and reread Ps. 93 until I had almost memorized it. I also read Ps. 96. Thinking on God bolstered my faith. He reigns! He is armed with strength. The more I thought on this, the more I could praise Him for what He was going to do. Throughout that day, when my mind returned to my need, I found myself enabled to praise Him with joy rather than request with doubt.

A week later I awakened with concerns heavy on my mind. At once, I knew that my strength was in returning to praise. My mind immediately went to those memorized phrases from Ps. 93. Once again God's Word lifted my spirit and my faith. I knew then that having Scripture available to feed on at all times was not an option for me if I wanted to live with confidence and joy. Having ready access to such verses provides a continual feast.

Without scripture for my mind to dwell on, my thoughts drift from praise to daydreaming, even worry. I want to have instant access to truth, so I can more nearly follow Paul's command to "Rejoice in the Lord always" (Phil. 4:4).

When we memorize scripture, we make it available to the Spirit to bring to our minds, especially for prayer and praise. There are additional benefits, however. The Psalmist said, "I have hidden your word in my heart that I might not sin against you" (119:11). There's no better way to keep us from sinning than to memorize God's Word. Even Jesus overcame temptation through memorized scripture (Matt. 4:4, 7, 10).

The best way to make a verse come alive in our spirits is to memorize it. As we go through the day reflecting on it, the Holy Spirit helps us understand what it means. "Reflect on what I am saying, for the Lord will give you insight into all of this" (2 Tim. 2:7). When we've tucked His words into the inner recesses of our hearts, God's Word comes to mind just at the moment when we need a promise or a command. We then gain understanding—practical knowledge of how to put the insight into practice.

One day while walking through our bedroom, I noticed the clutter piled on the dresser—books, unfiled articles, old receipts, a sweater, dust. God chose that moment to remind me of the verse I had been memorizing in Eph. 5:1—"Be imitators of God." The Spirit seemed to whisper, *If I were keeping house here, I wouldn't have that clutter. I'm a God of order. If you want to imitate Me, be a woman of order.*

Suddenly I found motivation to clean, and 45 minutes later our bedroom was ready for Jesus' inspection. Such moments provide a real payoff for memorizing. God invites us to hide His Word in our hearts so we can carry it with us through the day and let it live in us. Memorized words are more than words we can quote. They're words we can hear in our spirits and learn to obey. As we obey, we're filled with joy—the very purpose Jesus gave for His words. "I have told you this so that my joy may be in you and that your joy may be complete" (John 15:11).

One thing is necessary—we must have some Word in our minds to dwell on. If we can meditate only with an open Bible before us, how can we meditate day and night? We memorize to stock our minds with truth we can feed on at any time—today, next month, a year from now. When we "have all of them ready on [our] lips," the Holy Spirit has access to His Word.

Making It Ours

Our ability to memorize corresponds to our desire. We easily remember our addresses and phone numbers, and most housewives can recall bargain prices at the supermarket because we use these things. We make the effort to remember what's important to us.

Spare moments are like spare change, which adds up the longer we stash it away. If we choose to spend those moments on things that count for eternity, we'll have an investment of truth we could not have envisioned when we began. Most of us have several spare moments throughout our days, such as time spent waiting in lines or for appointments. Much of this can be used in memorization if we have verses with us. Then we can meditate day and night when we're driving the car or folding towels.

In deciding what to memorize, follow the hunger of your heart and the suggestion of the Spirit. If a passage has encouraged you, slowly repeat it to yourself while being attentive to God. It's important to keep that portion of Scripture before you throughout that day or the following days. Write out the verses on small cards, and strategically place them throughout your living space. Have the cards available where you get dressed, and take them with you throughout the day.

The three keys to memorizing are review, review, review—yet this need not be boring. When we take the words into ourselves, they continually surprise us with new truths.

After hearing someone say that if I read a passage of Scripture 50 times I would have it memorized, I decided to begin with Philippians. For several days I focused on rereading the first chapter. I had it very nearly memorized after the 50th reading. I started on the second chapter and began recording insights in my notebook. I noticed Paul's repeated exhortation to be joyful. On the sixth reading, I thought on Jesus' refusal to consider equality with God something to be grasped—a reminder not to consider an elevated position, special prominence, or special attention something to be grasped. The memorizing process was providing insights previously overlooked.

My dad was a farmer who occasionally served as a lay preacher in small local churches. In one service at which he was to speak, he put money in the offering, unaware that the offering would be given to him. At the close of the service, someone handed him the offering with the comment, "If you had put more into it, you would have gotten more out of it."

I thought of that comment during an early-morning Bible reading, so I decided to put more into it. I began memorizing the first few verses of 2 Cor. 4. At first I didn't find much for application, but I continued to memorize the verses as I had been taught to memorize piano music—repeating each phrase six times by memory, always including the beginning of the next phrase.

While saying the words, I let them filter through my thoughts. Did they give any direction or promise for today? Paul instructed Timothy, "Meditate upon these things; give thyself wholly to them" (1 Tim. 4:15, KJV). I tried to set my mind to gain understanding and to give myself wholly to the words.

Suddenly I understood how one phrase applied to me. As always when my search is rewarded, I realized that I was indebted to my Guide. "My Father in heaven has revealed this to you. You did not learn this from any human being" (Matt. 16:17, NLT).

My friend Nancy said that God told her during a fast to memorize scripture. Since then, memorizing has not been a burden. In fact, it's so satisfying to her that she feels she's eating delicious food. She loves using the memorized words in prayer. She doesn't try to learn whole chapters unless they're short, but she selects several verses that are meaningful to her. She reads the verses over and over many times until she can say them.

Memorize As You Can—Not As You Can't

Some may be tempted to say, "I simply can't memorize!" Perhaps no one tried harder but was unable to memorize than Ann Preston, the simple Irish lady mentioned earlier, who could read Scripture only after the Spirit taught her but could read nothing else. Because Ann was always pouring forth Scripture verses, many who knew her were surprised to know that one of Ann's sorest trials was her inability to memorize scripture.

One day Ann tried for an hour to memorize a verse, but she found it impossible to remember it. The next day she went over and over the same verse again but without success. Finally it seemed as though the voice spoke to her and asked, *Ann, what's the matter with you?*

Ann replied, "Well, I never saw the like of me. I spell and spell but can't remember a word." And she began to cry.

Her Father said, *Did you ever see a mother send a child on an errand and observe that the child forgot it before it got half way to its destination? Well, you would be just the same. But I'll give it to you just when I want you to have it, and then you won't have time to forget it.*[1]

Ann went beyond memorizing. She hungered for the Word and fed on it, and the Holy Spirit, who always makes up for our lack of abilities, made sure she "lacked no good thing." Our Lord who made us knows our limitations, and He's pleased when He sees us hungry enough for His Word to attempt memorization because we want it to live in our hearts.

When Paul prayed for those under his spiritual charge, his consistent request was that they would grow in knowledge. We'll look back on those periods in our lives when we were most sincere about memorizing and meditating on scripture and realize that they were the seasons we gained the most spiritual maturity.

Meditation

Brother Lawrence said, "Make thinking on God a holy habit." Memorized verses make this holy habit possible. The Scriptures will help you to know God if you meditate upon them throughout the day with a listening heart.

These Words Are Life

"Oh, how I love your law! I think about it all day long" (Ps. 119:97, NLT).

"It is pleasing when you keep them in your heart and have all of them ready on your lips" (Prov. 22:18).

"I have hidden your word in my heart that I might not sin against you" (Ps. 119:11).

"Reflect on what I am saying, for the Lord will give you insight into all this" (2 Tim. 2:7).

"I have told you this so that my joy may be in you and that your joy may be complete" (John 15:11).

"Jesus replied: 'Love the Lord your God with all your . . . mind'" (Matt. 22:37).

"Anyone who listens to the word but does not do what it says is like a man who looks at his face in a mirror and, after looking at himself, goes away and immediately forgets what he looks like. But the man who looks intently into the perfect law that gives freedom, and continues to do this, not forgetting what he has heard, but doing it—he will be blessed in what he does" (James 1:23-25).

What does the Spirit say to me through these words?

How will I respond?

Lord, I want to fill my mind with scripture so the Holy Spirit will again and again bring to my mind practical applications of Your truth.

8  Purpose-Driven Meditation

GOD GAVE MOSES A CLEAR COMMAND AND A PROMISE. What promise could be better than the one He attached to this command?— "Meditate on [the book of the Law] . . . day and night. . . . Then you will be prosperous and successful" (Josh. 1:8).

At least that was how I selectively read it for many years. Then I noticed the key phrase. "Meditate . . . so that you may be careful to do everything written in it. Then you will be prosperous and successful" (Josh. 1:8).

God does not attach His promise to the simple process of meditation but to the process of considering Scripture so we can continually live by it.

Biblical meditation comes from a Greek word meaning "to revolve in the mind." It bears little resemblance to Eastern forms of meditation, whose purpose is to train the consciousness to move beyond thoughts, words, and images to a kind of "emptiness." Rather than emptying our minds of words and images, we take in the Word and feed on it. Meditation helps us absorb scriptural truth on a deep level. And when we do, we agree with the psalmist: "Oh, how I love your law! I meditate on it all day long" (Ps. 119:97).

In meditation we go over the Word in our minds, asking *What does this mean?* We hold it questioningly before the Teacher, and as a result we gain fresh understanding. E. E. Shelhammer said the early saints made much of solitude accompanied by godly meditation. The results? "They were deep thinkers; we are imitators."[1] Even our Bible study may have us merely thinking thoughts from others rather than hearing from God.

We also gain a spirit of worship through meditation. In Ps. 77 we find the psalmist in the depths of despair. "Will the Lord reject us forever? Will he never show his favor again?" (v. 7). Then he begins to meditate, and those discouraging thoughts fly out the window: "I will meditate on all your works and consider all your mighty deeds" (v. 12). He then begins: "Your ways, O God, are holy. What god is so great as our God? You are the God who performs miracles; you display your power among the peoples" (vv. 13-14). He ends with "You led your people like a flock." Meditation on God's greatness and answered prayers was David's way to begin singing a new song.

Practicing the art of meditation

The image of a cow chewing its cud is often used to describe the practice of meditation. First the cow goes out and gets some grass, sits down, chews it for a while, and then swallows it. A little later the cow reprocesses its cud, chews some more, then swallows again. We can visualize the cow processing and reprocessing the food until it's fully digested.

Our meditation involves taking in the bread of God's Word and "chewing" on it by reading and thinking about it. It then sinks down into our hearts as we go about other things. Later that day, we bring it back to our minds and reflect on it some more. Meditation is taking in the bread of God's Word, chewing on it, and digesting it until it becomes a part of who we are. While we meditate, the Word becomes so pleasant that we fully agree with the psalmist, "The law from your mouth is more precious to me than thousands of pieces of silver and gold" (Ps. 119:72).

Meditation begins as we read, listening with all our hearts. It requires that we pay attention to the details of scripture, but it's different from Bible study. In Bible study we analyze the text; in scripture meditation we take pleasure in scripture and enter into it. Then we carry His Words—perhaps just a phrase from our reading—in our minds, pondering, *How can I live this? What is God saying?* We bring the scripture to our minds throughout the day, thinking on it, alert for ways to apply His words.

Every word "is inspired by God and is useful to teach us what is true and to make us realize what is wrong in our lives. It straightens us out and teaches us to do what is right. It is God's way of preparing us in every way, fully equipped for every good thing God wants us to do" (2 Tim. 3:16-17, NLT). These words explain why God can promise success and prosperity if we continually keep His words before us, seeking to live by them.

Enjoy a Perpetual Feast

Samuel Logan Brengle, a favorite preacher in the early days of the Salvation Army, formed a habit of choosing a text for his day. As a traveler stuffs snacks in his pockets, Brengle daily stuffed the pockets of his mind with tasty treats from the Word. These snacks were short, simple statements of promise, reassurance, or comfort that he would turn to for support through the day.

Once Brengle wrote to his wife about a text that described one day's meditation. Notice his use of reflecting, imagining, and personalizing. He obviously enjoyed this practice.

My text this A.M. was "Thy testimonies are my delight and my counselors." The word "counselors" struck me. The Psalmist sits down and talks over his affairs with God's testimonies and finds out what they have to say. Think of sitting down with Abraham when Lot chooses Sodom and the rich valley or with Isaac when he surrenders his wells to the Philistines, and talking over the advisability of being meek and yielding to others; or with Job on his ash heap, and talking about trusting God in affliction; or with Paul in the Philippian jail, and talking about rejoicing in tribulation; or with Joseph or Daniel or David. Bless God! That is just what I do when I sit down to meditate upon and take counsel from God's testimonies."[2]

Sometimes even meditating on just one memorized phrase can radically adjust our thinking. One mother said her daughter Karen was suddenly seized by an attack of stage fright the afternoon of the school play. She thought of suggesting that Karen study her lines some more but instead suggested that they take a silent walk, meditating on "Thou wilt keep him in perfect peace, whose mind is stayed on thee" (Isa. 26:3, KJV). When they got home, Karen was relaxed and the stage fright gone.

The week I focused on Ps. 93, The Weather Channel was filled with news of Hurricane Isabel. I thought often on verses 3 and 4:

The mighty oceans have roared, O LORD. The mighty oceans roar like thunder; the mighty oceans roar as they pound the shore.

But mightier than the violent raging of the seas, mightier than the breakers on the shore—the LORD above is mightier than these! (NLT).

I wrote in my journal, "I meditate on these verses and my mountain shrinks into a mole hill." How pleasant it is to meditate upon His goodness, to allow our thoughts to dwell upon what He's done, upon His magnificence! "When I am preoccupied with the truth of God and His sovereign plans for me, all thoughts of discontent fly away—almost the instant I choose to meditate on God," Jan Winebrenner said.[3]

One morning recently my husband read to me from Dan. 6, and we decided to take verse 16 with us through the day: "May your God, whom you serve continually, rescue you." Different times we mentioned the verse. We thought of it in prayer. We thought of it when we remembered our son was driving a long distance. The Lord we serve continually would rescue him from danger.

God intends for us to enjoy our tasty snack at His table more than our Snickers bar or Starbucks latte during break. "How sweet are your words to my taste, sweeter than honey to my mouth!" (Ps. 119:103).

When we set our minds on His thoughts, fully intending to respond to every word, we can expect to be blessed. For the Lover of our souls, we're receiving truth that feeds our spirits. "I stand at the door and knock" (Rev. 3:20), Jesus says to us believers desiring a perpetual feast in the inner sanctuary of our hearts. Meditation opens the door and makes our hearts a portable sanctuary for this inner feast.

MEDITATION

The Word of God brings forth God's purposes in us when we soak in the passage and find joy in responding to it. Take a few minutes as you read these verses to consider how your life would benefit if you viewed Scripture meditation as these writers did.

These Words Are Life

"I reflect at night on who you are, O LORD, and I obey your law because of this" (Ps. 119:55, NLT).

"Study this Book of the Law continually. Meditate on it day and night so you may be sure to obey all that is written in it. Only then will you succeed" (Josh. 1:8, NLT).

"Oh, the joys of those who . . . delight in doing everything the LORD wants. Day and night they think about his law" (Ps. 1:1-2, NLT).

"Oh, how I love your law! I meditate on it all day long. Your commands make me wiser than my enemies, for they are ever with me. I have more insight than all my teachers, for I meditate on your statutes" (Ps. 119:97-99).

"If ye know these things, happy are ye if ye do them" (John 13:17, KJV).

"Meditate upon these things; give thyself wholly to them; that thy profiting may appear to all" (1 Tim. 4:15, KJV).

What does the Spirit say to me through these words?

How will I respond?

Help me, Lord, to show You that I long to obey Your Word by taking time for unbroken, serious reflection.

9 Be Cleansed by the Word

WE ARE "CLEAN BECAUSE OF THE WORD" (John 15:3), Jesus states, and if we could glimpse the love behind the Word, we would not fear coming to it. God uses His Word to cleanse us and to re-shape us into the kind of people He wants us to be, but He may do it differently than we anticipate. He "does not treat us as our sins deserve or repay us according to our iniquities" (Ps. 103:10). He does not shove us away because we've failed. He's a loving Father who patiently deals with us as His dear children.

When we've disobeyed God's law we are apt to expect His Word to come as a club, but then we find He speaks tenderly and gently. "Let my teaching fall like rain and my words descend like dew" (Deut. 32:2). His teaching is refreshing, reinvigorating, watering us in our dryness. His speech settles gently on our spirits like dew.

Nancy met Don soon after she and her husband moved to a new town. One day when the phone rang, expecting her husband's voice, she said, "Robert . . ."[1]

Instead of her hearing her husband, however, she heard a deep voice that she instantly recognized as Don's. "I wish!" he exclaimed.

Nancy murmured, "Don, don't say that."

"Why not?" he replied.

Although Nancy quickly changed the subject and took care

of the reason for his call, this exchange began a battle in Nancy's mind. About two months after that phone call, Nancy and her husband invited several people over. She didn't mingle much with Don that night, but the few times they were together, the sparks of physical attraction flew.

That night while in bed, Nancy crossed the moral line in her thought life, opening the door to temptation. Within weeks, Don filled her thoughts day and night.

After struggling with indecent thoughts for nearly six months, Nancy attended a prayer retreat. Her reserve broke, and she wept openly as she confessed to a small group that she struggled with temptation.

Unexpectedly when she was alone that afternoon, the Lord began to sweetly minister to her spirit. Instead of condemnation, Nancy experienced His tender words falling like dew on her spirit as Ps. 23:1-2 and Matt. 11:28 played over and over in her mind. "The Lord is my shepherd. . . . He leadeth me beside the still waters," and "Come unto me, all ye that labour and are heavy laden, and I will give you rest" (KJV).

During the following weeks, when Nancy was plagued by thoughts of Don, she had a new strength and perseverance. She began using scripture as she prayed: "Set your mind on things above, not on earthly things" (Col. 3:2) and "Whatever is pure . . . think about such things" (Phil. 4:8). Slowly but surely she "purified [herself] by obeying the truth" (1 Pet. 1:22).

Nancy escaped the treacherous pit of immoral thinking because she had a humble spirit—the first requisite for receiving the cleansing the Word provides. She confessed before others her need. "I will bless those who have humble and contrite hearts" (Isa. 66:2, NLT), God promises.

Be Washed by the Word

"Place a laver [a fountain made out of brass mirrors] at the entrance of the tabernacle," God instructed Moses. Before the priests could enter the Holy Place, they had to use this laver to wash their hands and feet, because they could not enter God's presence with any spot on them. In fact, the punishment for doing so would be serious: "Whenever they enter the Tent of Meeting, they shall wash with water so that they will not die" (Exod. 30:20). Quite a severe penalty!

The message to us is this: "We have no fellowship with God with sin in our lives. Just as the priests could not be in God's presence if there was a spot upon them, we, too, cannot maintain our communion with the Lord unless we maintain personal holiness.

Fortunately, we have a laver—the Word of God. We're "wash[ed] of water by the word" (Eph. 5:26, KJV), Paul says, meaning that we look into the Word (the mirror where we see ourselves), and the Word washes us and changes our minds. It's wonderful that the Bible, which corrects and reproves us, is also the fountain of cleansing. We must simply follow James' advice to "Humbly accept the message God has planted in [our] hearts" (James 1:21, NLT). He tells us plainly how to be washed by the Word:

Don't fool yourself into thinking that you are a listener when you are anything but, letting the Word go in one ear and out the other. *Act* on what you hear! Those who hear and don't act are like those who glance in the mirror, walk away, and two minutes later have no idea who they are, what they look like (1:22-24, TM).

One of the reasons we fail to be cleansed by the Word is that we have some point of disobedience we refuse to acknowledge. Rather than acting on what we hear, our defenses guard these blind spots. We may memorize, "Don't just pretend that you love others" (Rom. 12:9, NLT), but we don't dwell on the words long enough for the Spirit to point out the times our love has been superficial or when we've pretended to love and yet had self-interest in our actions.

Or perhaps we fool ourselves into thinking that we're listeners when we are not, because we listen for others rather than for ourselves. George Muller observed that we're apt to read the Word and think about others' needs rather than ponder it for ourselves. Parents read it for their children, evangelists read it for their congregations, and teachers read it for their students. "Read the Word of God always with reference to your own heart," Muller advises.

Another reason we fail to be cleansed by the Word is that we have some point of disobedience we refuse to acknowledge — a sort of prickly porcupine tucked away in a corner of our heart. We believe we're filled with love, and most of our heart is. But when someone who has wronged us comes to mind or when another person receives the special prominence we had desired, do we eagerly receive God's definition of love? "Love is patient, love is kind. It does not envy, it does not boast, it is not proud" (1 Cor. 13:4).

When God speaks to us, the first thing He asks is that we do not harden our hearts but "humbly accept the word planted in [us]" (James 1:21). Without a tender, humble spirit, we go backward spiritually no matter how much we fill our heads and mouths with Bible knowledge. "If you hear his voice, do not harden your hearts" (Heb. 3:15), God said not to unbelievers but to believers.

Be Submissive to the Word

Learning to be cleansed by the Word is not a mystical process. One of the functions of the Holy Spirit is to bring to our remembrance the words of Christ (John 14:26). When we fill our minds with scripture, the Holy Spirit will again and again bring to our minds practical applications of His truth. It's not always easy to submit to the Word, but as we do He gives us grace to accept His cleansing.

"Those whom I love, I rebuke and discipline," the Lord promises in Rev. 3:19, addressing Christians. Then He adds, "I stand at the door and knock" (v. 20). When God knocks on a certain area in our lives, we can either submit to His discipline or refuse it.

The psalmist wrote of the importance of speedy obedience. "I made haste, and delayed not to keep thy commandments" (Ps. 119:60, KJV). A glimpse of how we can follow God's Word more closely may be with us only long enough for us to decide whether we'll obey it or disregard it.

When Jesus called the disciples, it seems as though He said, "Follow me" and walked on. They could follow or be left behind. The Book of Amos implies that at times it appears truth can be surrendered to and followed, or the opportunity and grace to respond may be gone once we turn away.

One evening while reading the evening paper, the husband of one of the ladies in our Bible study suggested to his wife, "How about inviting my parents to visit us this weekend? They need a few days away from home."

With her hands in soapsuds and her back to her husband, she groaned inwardly as she reviewed the weekend schedule. Their visit would not fit into her plans at all. Before she replied, a phrase from Isaiah came to mind: "Hide not thyself from thine own flesh" (58:7, KJV).

She had a choice. Would she ignore this command and convince herself that it didn't apply to this situation? Or would she choose to be cleansed by the Word? She chose quickly before her good intentions could go down the drain with the soapsuds. "Sure—go ahead and invite them," she responded.

With a cleansed attitude, she was free to enjoy that weekend, trusting God to arrange their schedules. Memories of attending an organ concert, buying donuts at midnight, and talking together as they worked in the kitchen lingered as pleasant reminders that there's joy in obeying the Word.

Our response to the Word is our response to God. When we humbly accept His cleansing Word, His grace changes our lives.

Meditation

Reading the Word so it changes our lives is more than another program for self-improvement. It's God's way to cleanse us from our sins and faults—past and present. If you have a sin from which you long to be free, ask the Spirit to lead you to the Word, which will cleanse you.

These Words Are Life

"You have purified yourselves by obeying the truth" (1 Pet. 1:22).

"Ye are clean through the word which I have spoken unto you" (John 15:3, KJV).

"Christ also loved the church . . . that he might sanctify and cleanse it with the washing of water by the word" (Eph. 5:25-26, KJV).

"I made haste, and delayed not to keep thy commandments" (Ps. 119:60, KJV).

"Now if you obey me fully and keep my covenant, then out of all nations you will be my treasured possession. . . . . You will be for me a kingdom of priests and a holy nation." (Exod. 19:5-6).

Every word "is inspired by God and is useful to teach us what is true and to make us realize what is wrong in our lives. It straightens us out and teaches us to do what is right. It is God's way of preparing us in every way, fully equipped for every good thing God wants us to do" (2 Tim. 3:16-17, NLT).

"The laws of the LORD . . . are a warning to those who hear them; there is great reward for those who obey them" (Ps. 19:9, 11, NLT).

"Receive with meekness the engrafted word, which is able to save your souls" (James 1:21, KJV).

What does the Spirit say to me through these words?

How will I respond?

Lord, thank You for Your gentle Holy Spirit, who reveals my blind spots and areas of inconsistencies when I read Your Word. Make me clean through obedience to Your Truth.

10 When Your Mind Wanders

JEWISH PHILOSOPHER AND THEOLOGIAN MARTIN BUBER has suggested that the name of God usually translated as "I am who I am," might better be translated as "I will be present (to you) as I will be present (to you.)" He was promising to be fully present.[1] God is here for us; He is fully present when we open our Bibles. Just remembering that truth makes me want to be fully present also.

Without doubt, though, wandering thoughts will plague us. Missionary J. Hudson Taylor found that the hardest part of a missionary career was to have undistracted regular, prayerful Bible study. "Satan will always find you something to do," he would say, "when you ought to be occupied about that, if it is only arranging a window blind."

Even John Wesley admitted in his journal that he experienced dry times in his devotions. Probably all of us will admit that at times our meditations have been lifeless and empty and that we have fallen asleep while reading. We seek to concentrate, to be open to the Word. We read a verse, then reread it, and suddenly discover that our mind is on the phone call we need to make. We turn two pages in the Bible and realize we've read nothing.

One thing is certain. We will not be able to read the Bible with the same intensity every time. Some days even forcing ourselves to dutifully read will be a struggle. What's going on in our lives greatly affects our ability to stay with our reading. Yet whenever great distracters come—a move, vacation, illness, family trauma—we can persistently keep that time set apart for hearing God knowing that eventually we will once again hear His voice.

Overcoming Distractions

Rather than being afraid of distractions, the Lord wants us to learn how to manage and even overcome them. When memories or thoughts arise during our Bible reading, we can allow these distractions to become a part of our dialogue with God. For instance, if our minds wander to someone we're concerned about, we can turn the scripture into prayer for that person, and then our time will not be wasted.

I often find it helpful to keep a things-to-do pad with me and simply jot down the tasks that are vying for my attention. I can then return to my reading and focus on the scripture. Usually I end up with a list of things to do I might have otherwise neglected.

In his book *Shaped by the Word*, Mulholland suggests that while in prayer we not fight the experience of thinking about last night's television show or the meeting coming up or the children who need braces:

> Your resistance will just make your inattention stronger. Instead, calmly, steadily, gently but persistently return to the text. . . . If you again find yourself going off in another direction, just firmly return to the text and begin reading again. As often as distractions intrude or your attention wanders, return to the text . . . and to being still before the Word. If you are persistent, gradually you will develop the ability to still yourself and to "be there" with God.[2]

Peter's words guide us: "Prepare your minds for action; be self-controlled" (1 Pet. 1:13). If we determine to give our whole attention to what we read, we'll find that the Holy Spirit gives us grace to refuse to chase every thought that beckons. "Set your minds on things above" (Col. 3:2), Paul says, implying that it's possible for us to do that. Sometimes I find I have to set my mind on what I'm reading, set it again, and then yet again because my mind is so prone to wander off.

Concentrating our minds with the strictest self-control may include finding a quiet place to read. Being attentive always involves quieting ourselves before God, and we're more likely to do that when we avoid distractions. To be quiet means our eyes are on Him and we're fully present before the One who is fully present for us.

Mary sat quietly at Jesus' feet, while Martha kept on working. Perhaps Martha could have overheard Jesus as she prepared the meal, but her mind would not have been fully engaged, fully intent on His Words. Her main concern was the meal preparation. This type of listening was unsatisfactory to Mary. She wanted to be fully present when Jesus spoke. Nothing replaces the quiet sitting at His feet while we ignore the duties that others make priorities. "I wait quietly before God" (Ps. 62:1, NLT).

We're perhaps most easily distracted when we're "meeting a habit" rather than meeting God. If we recognize that our devotions are perfunctory, we must begin where we are and pray, *God, give me the desire to hear You.* Jesus knows we're like sheep that, once they're on their backs, are helpless to roll over by themselves. Our Shepherd understands our helplessness and will surprise us with His ready response. He has an abundance of ways to encourage us to be faithful. Sometimes we simply forget to ask. Rely on His faithfulness to help you, not on your own faithfulness to do your best at all times.

At times changing the pattern of our devotions may help us maintain interest. George Mueller habitually had begun his morning devotions with prayer and would spend almost all of his time until breakfast in prayer. But His mind often wandered for the first 15 to 30 minutes. Then he began listening to God speak through the Word before praying. As he read and meditated, searching every verse for blessing, he would find himself turning what he read into prayer. His mind stopped wandering almost immediately.

Faithfulness Counts

God richly rewards those who are faithful during what seem to be unproductive times. Judy remembers one particularly dark time. "I couldn't pray, and I couldn't find anything in Scripture. It frightened me, because the silence was so severe. I searched for days and found nothing. I finally realized that this could go on forever. I told the Lord that I was going to trust Him to take care of me. This lasted for nine months. I prayed. I read, I took care of my children, I went to church—but there was nothing from God; absolutely nothing." Judy did her best to praise Him despite her dryness. At the end of the ninth month, she was dutifully thanking God when all of a sudden He broke through her darkness. Judy sensed God's immense pleasure in her faithfulness.

It's in these dry times that we can more easily offer to God a "costly gift." In his book *Spiritual Progress* Fenelon writes, "The will to love God is the whole of religion."

God knows exactly how much we love Him by observing our determination, the set of our wills. Sometimes we go to the Word simply because we've deliberately chosen to faithfully spend time in scripture. Such reading may seem unsatisfactory to us at times, but it is very pleasing to God.

Much of our true spiritual development comes during the dry and hard times. God forbid, to modify David's words, that we give Him *devotions* that cost us nothing.

God Knows Our Limits

Becky and I meet regularly to talk about what Jesus is doing in our lives. She's a wife, a mother of three, and a physician, and one recent week had been particularly stressful. As we sat down at the table, Becky explained the brief entries she had made in her notebook. "This was a two-mites week," she said, referring to our earlier discussion of the widow who presented her tiny gift at the Temple.

Jesus had been unimpressed as He observed the rich people proudly drop their coins into the collection box. Then a poor widow came by and dropped in two mites; some versions call it two pennies. The two mites appeared totally inadequate to those hanging around watching, but Jesus knew her limits. With what must have been great fondness in His voice, He said to those close enough to hear, "This poor widow has given more than all the rest of them. For they have given a tiny part of their surplus, but she, poor as she is, has given everything she has" (Luke 21:3-4, NLT).

Just as Jesus completely understood the widow's abilities to give, He also knows our abilities. He understands when we feel emotionally low and spiritually drained or when our days are overflowing with interruptions. On those days we do our two-cents' worth, and Jesus looks on with love and says, "But she, poor as she is, has given everything she has." Our gifts to God, both in time, money, and emotional strength, are measured by our reserves. God loves it when we give Him the devotion that costs all we have.

"Pray as you can, not as you can't," someone once said. The same goes for Bible reading—read as you can, not as you can't. Reading when we just can't seem to set our minds on things above has its value.

One night I stayed up to spend time with the Lord but soon went to sleep on my knees. I awoke and thought of going to bed but decided, "No, I'll try again." Again I went to sleep. When I awoke, I gave up and went to bed. The next morning the Lord was near, helping me to pray. He seemed to say, *I saw your efforts last night and am rewarding you for it.* God notices our efforts to draw near to Him even when we've felt they might have been a waste of time or simply a routine. He interprets them as desire.

"Come near to God and he will come near to you" (James 4:8)—eventually, if not today.

MEDITATION

Have you ever been eager to share some news with a friend but realized that he or she only appeared to be attentive? How disappointing to realize your friend's mind was elsewhere! Could it be that the Holy Spirit is disappointed when we read without being attentively present to God?

These Words Are Life

"Come here and listen to me! I'll pour out the spirit of wisdom upon you and make you wise" (Prov. 1:23, NLT).

"Be still, and know that I am God" (Ps. 46:10).

"Set your minds on things above, not on earthly things" (Col. 3:2).

"Prepare your minds for action; be self-controlled" (1 Pet. 1:13).

"He let you hear his voice from heaven so he could instruct you" (Deut. 4:36, NLT).

"I wait quietly before God" (Ps. 62:1, NLT).

"Make every effort to add to your . . . knowledge, self-control; and to self-control, perseverance" (2 Pet. 1:5-6).

"Do not be afraid, Daniel. Since the first day that you set your mind to gain understanding and to humble yourself before your God, your words were heard, and I have come in response to them" (Dan. 10:12).

What does the Spirit say to me through these words?

How will I respond?

Lord, teach me to ignore distractions and to acknowledge Your presence when I open my Bible.

11 Have a Routine

HAVE YOU EVER BEEN TEMPTED to find a word from the Lord to apply to your immediate needs by simply opening the Bible and reading randomly? I don't recommend this method, but I do recall a few times when God mercifully let me hear a Word in that way. When my husband, Daniel, was about to begin his third year of medical school, we knew he would have to be on call at night sometimes, leaving me alone as often as every third night. I was terrified by the thought of staying alone. We began praying that I would not be afraid those nights he had to stay at the med center.

The first night Daniel was on call, I happened to open my Bible to Proverbs and read, "When thou liest down, thou shalt not be afraid: yea, thou shalt lie down, and thy sleep shall be sweet" (3:24, KJV). That verse proved to be absolutely true. When I would lie down, I was not afraid. One night I heard a noise outside, and, remembering—and believing—my verse, I hurriedly hopped in bed. Sure enough, I was not afraid and went right to sleep.

Sometimes God does speak to us like that, but a better habit is to read according to a routine and expect the Lord to give us what we need in that passage. One day I desired God's blessing in a certain situation and wondered if I should fast breakfast and lunch. I knew the Spirit would lead me. In morning devotions our daughter read Ps. 37, and I took the phrase "Wait on the LORD" as my answer. I would fast to tell the Lord I was waiting on Him.

The next morning I opened to Isaiah thinking, *I really haven't been getting much out of these chapters.* I was tempted to skip to another book but stuck to reading Isaiah. When I came to 25:9, I knew God had this special promise there for me that day: "Lo, this is our God; we have waited for him, and he will save us: this is the LORD; we have waited for him, we will be glad and rejoice in his salvation."

God sees our walking in the path of duty—the routine—as faithfulness, and He responds to it. The busier we are, the more important it is that we have some methods in place.

What to Read

George Muller, who read the entire Bible more than 100 times, advised reading the Old Testament and, after a chapter or two, placing a mark there and reading a chapter or two the next day in the New Testament. His method was to continue alternating between the Old and New Testaments.

John Wesley suggested that in each day's reading, "if you have leisure, to read a chapter out of the Old, and one out of the New Testament: if you cannot do this, to take a single chapter, or a part of one." G. Campbell Morgan counseled his readers to begin with the Gospels.

Your personal spiritual needs will often determine what you read. For instance, if you lack assurance of salvation, Tim La-Haye suggests reading 1 John every day for 30 days. If your faith is low, read the Gospel of John: "These are written that you may believe" (John 20:31). When going through difficulties, spend time in reading God's promises in the Psalms. As someone said, "There's a psalm for every sigh."

Ask the Holy Spirit to direct you as you select a book to read. He will lead you into the correct portion for this time of your life. Once you begin, believe that you chose correctly, and read each day expecting to find what you need for that day.

If you're not reading from Genesis to Revelation, keep a page in your notebook where you record the book you've read and the date you finished it. A glance at this periodically will help you to eventually cover the entire Bible.

John Wesley seems to indicate that we should work with fairly small units of Scripture. The lectionary that is printed in the back of this book is helpful in doing this, because it preselects usually rather brief portions.

In addition to regular Bible reading, some people read the psalm that correspond to the date and then read additional psalms in increments of 30, 60, and 90. For example, on the first day of the month you would read Ps. 1, 31, 61, 91, and 121. Many read the chapter of Proverbs that corresponds to the date.

Phillip Henry had a novel idea for daily meditation. Two hundred years ago, he advised his children to take a verse of Ps. 119 every morning to meditate on, and so go over the Psalm twice in the year. "That will bring you to be in love with all the rest of the Scriptures," he promised. This may explain why his son Matthew loved the Word so much that he wrote the Matthew Henry Commentaries that we still use today.[1] (Every verse of Ps. 119 contains one of ten words for "instruction," with the exception of vv. 84 and 122.)

Since we're reading not for quantity but for changed lives, we don't need to cover a given amount of text. Perhaps you can relate to D. L. Moody, who said he used to read a certain number of chapters a day but that if someone had asked him two hours later what he had read, he could not have told him. When he was a boy, Moody used to hoe corn on a farm. In order to cover a lot of ground, he hoed it so quickly that at night he had to place a stick in the ground to be able to tell where he had stopped when he came out the next morning. "That," he said, "was somewhat in the same fashion as running through so many chapters every day."[2]

If we find ourselves in a holding pattern over one phrase, verse, or even a chapter, we won't be concerned with how quickly we get through the Book. So what if it takes us two years or even three? Our hunger is to experience Paul's words: "Let the words of Christ, in all their richness, live in your hearts and make you wise" (Col. 3:16, NLT).

We may often find it to be much more satisfying to our spirit to feast on five verses than to read with little gained in five chapters. If we read just a small portion, eager to be shaped by it, and spend time thinking on it, along with taking notes, we can more easily carry that part of the Word and meditate on it throughout the day.

When to Read

Although it's possible to fully concentrate when other people are around, it's not easy. If practical, it's best to read when alone. When God wanted to speak in a life-changing way to Moses, He called him to come to the top of the mountain. No one was to be near who would interfere with Moses' ability to hear the voice of God (Exod. 34:2-8).

Our efforts to find a time and place when and where we can listen to God without distractions will tell something of the intensity of our desire to hear Him. Many experienced Christians advise us to give God the best time of our day, not the dregs. Although some of us are "morning persons" and some are "night owls," most of us do better if we start our day with at least some nourishment. Similarly, feeding on a word from God will provide strength for the day ahead.

George Muller learned that his first need in the day was to fellowship with God: "Since God has taught me this point, it is as plain to me as anything that the first thing the child of God has to do morning by morning is to obtain food for his inner man. As the outward man is not fit for work for any length of time except we take food, and as this is one of the first things we do in the morning, so it should be with the inner man."

We will not always meet with God at the same time in different stages of our lives. A disciplined life allows flexibility, and God will give us grace to find the time that is right for us. The days of caring for my mother during her terminal illness were too full to allow for the blocks of time I needed to be alone with the Lord. Before going to sleep at night, I would often say, *Please, Jesus, wake me up tonight to spend time with You.* I would be surprisingly wide awake when He awakened me.

He continues to do that when I ask Him. The phone doesn't ring between 2 and 4 A.M., and distractions are minimal then. The time is God's, and I've found myself looking forward to going to bed in anticipation of those nighttime awakenings.

God's perfect ways are as varied as His people. William Law (1686-1761) was a contemplative, mystical recluse who said that we may change the timing and hours of "our devotions to the conditions of our lives and the state of our hearts." God will give you the time that best fits you and your schedule.

One of Ruth Graham's daughters told her mother that she had no time for devotions because of caring for her children. Her mother wisely counseled her to use those moments when rocking a baby, changing a diaper, or washing dishes to worship the Lord. God can be a part of our routine in any season of life when our hearts hunger for Him.

While we can never be legalistic in the area of spiritual disciplines, we must resist with all our strength the temptation to make our spiritual reading a lesser priority in our daily routine. We may have to learn to say a polite "no" to extra unnecessary work, television programs, and magazines. Our "no" to these will be a "yes" to something of greater value.

MEDITATION

Our lives change when we have a loving relationship with God and offer our obedience because we want to please Him. To do this, we will not treat His Word in a casual, offhand manner. The following verses describe a proper desire for regular times with our God.

These Words Are Life

"Teach us to make the most of our time, so that we may grow in wisdom" (Ps. 90:12, NLT).

"Do your best to present yourself to God as one approved, a workman who does not need to be ashamed and who correctly handles the word of truth" (2 Tim. 2:15).

"Let the words of Christ, in all their richness, live in your hearts and make you wise" (Col. 3:16, NLT).

"Draw close to God, and God will draw close to you" (James 4:8, NLT).

"The fruit of the Spirit is . . . faithfulness . . . self-control" (Gal. 5:22-23).

"Now when Daniel learned that the decree had been published, he went home to his upstairs room where the windows opened toward Jerusalem. Three times a day he got down on his knees and prayed, giving thanks to his God, just as he had done before" (Dan. 6:10).

What does the Spirit say to me through these words?

How will I respond?

Lord, may my spiritual hungering and thirsting be as real and as consistent as my physical hungering and thirsting.

12 Let the Word Change Your Prayer Life

"I COULD NEVER MEMORIZE SCRIPTURE until I began praying God's Word," my neighbor Janet said, mentioning one of the blessings of using God's Word in prayer. But there are many more.

When we feel too distressed or too distracted to find the right words to take to God, we can open our Bibles, call to Him using His own words, and find it marvelously satisfying. D. L. Moody declared that he knew of no sweeter experience than kneeling down and pleading the promise he had found. At times it seems that Spirit-inspired words take us into His presence quickly and almost effortlessly.

The promises of God nourish our faith. When He first called Abraham, He inundated his soul with a sea of promises. He spoke to him from the starry heavens, and Abraham saw great possibilities of things for himself and his descendants. He drank in God's promises until his faith became powerful, even before any of them were fulfilled. God deals with us similarly. When He wants to use us or give answers to our prayers, He begins by opening up to us the promises in His Word and the possibilities they offer.

I often find that I can't truly believe God is hearing and will answer my prayer until I focus on a Scripture verse. So as I pray, I ask the Lord, *What specifically should I pray? Give me Your Word to believe for this situation.* Frequently the Holy Spirit brings a verse to mind that exactly speaks the language of my

79

heart. While I think on the verse, it is as though my faith has found a resting place. Later, when I recall the need for which I've prayed, I can also recall the promise I'm trusting God to fulfill. Giving thanks for the fulfillment of His Word strengthens my ability to continue believing.

The more we use Scripture in prayer, the more our faith will grow. "Faith comes from listening to this message of good news—the Good News about Christ" (Rom. 10:17, NLT). We're told to take "the sword of the Spirit, which is the word of God. And pray in the Spirit on all occasions" (Eph. 6:17-18). The implication here is that we are to take the Word of God with us when we expect to pray in the Spirit.

Andrew Murray taught that much of the Word with little prayer gives a sickly spiritual life, while much prayer with little of the Word gives more life but little steadfastness. A healthy prayer life involves combining the Word with prayer.[1]

The Absolute Dependability of the Word

We use scripture in prayer because of the absolute dependability of His Word. All that God has said is reliable. In the Hebrew there is no special term for "promise." "Promise" is simply "word." God's Word is His promise. With God no more is needed. He is so loving, so powerful, and so unchangeable that a word is enough. His Word is power, because it is Truth.

Jesus said, "Until heaven and earth disappear, not the smallest letter, not the least stroke of a pen, will by any means disappear from the Law until everything is accomplished" (Matt. 5:18). Words of comfort or assurance God has given you will endure forever. Someday we'll exclaim, "Not one word has failed of all the good promises he gave" (1 Kings 8:56).

"The eyes of the LORD keep watch over knowledge," He assures us in Prov. 22:12. Because God personally sees that His Word accomplishes His desires, why not reverently quote it back to Him?

At the top of one of the typed pages of Scripture verses I take with me to prayer, I've written God's promise in Jer. 1:12—"I am watching to see that my word is fulfilled." The literal fulfillment of some of the verses I have prayed has surprised me. For instance, my husband asked me to pray Paul's prayer for Philemon: "I pray that you may be active in sharing your faith" (Philem. 6). After I began regularly praying that prayer, he told me of new opportunities to witness, one time to nearly 70 people in one setting.

When God gives His Word, it is more than simply a piece of information; it is His will in a particular situation. So we can go to God as the psalmist did and say, "Remember your promise to me, for it is my only hope" (119:49).

When His promise is our only hope, we are not hopeless! We find comfort in His promises and are to take them to prayer. God delights in our turning His promises into confident requests: *Lord, You have made this promise, and You cannot deny Your truth.*

God highly regards his Word. "Thou hast magnified thy word above all thy name" (Ps. 138:2, KJV). He is pleased when our view of His Word reflects His view.

Praying Inspired Words

Many of the Psalms were originally written as prayers. When we read them as prayers, we discover that they draw us into God's presence. For instance, turn Ps. 145 into a prayer or even a song, and it will encourage your faith.

Often prayers in the Psalms help us identify our specific needs when we pray them as if they were our own deepest prayers. One lady says that each week she selects a Psalm and then daily takes a few moments to pray through it. She tries to live with it, returning to it each day, praying it as if it were her own prayer—whispering its pleas for help or joining in its praise and worship. Slowly the Psalm becomes her prayer.

Eavesdrop on some of the most significant prayers ever prayed, and you'll notice that men such as David were preoccupied with God's character. Borrow their inspired words as you pray, "Yours, O LORD, is the greatness and the power and the glory and the majesty and the splendor, for everything in heaven and earth is yours. Yours, O LORD, is the kingdom; you are exalted as head over all" (1 Chron. 29:11-12). Our faith grows as we meditate on God's ultimate control.

God delights in prayers we pray repeatedly that are based on His Word. Phoebe Palmer, a Methodist leader in the 1800s, began each day by praying for each member of her family individually, pleading the promise of Isa. 44:3 — "I will pour out my Spirit upon thy seed, and my blessing upon thine offspring" (KJV).

Dick Eastman wrote in *The University of the Word* that he had prayed daily a specific prayer for his family based on Luke 2:52. He prayed, *Lord, help my family to grow mentally (in wisdom), physically (in stature), spiritually (with favor toward God), and socially (with favor toward people)."* After seven years, God graciously revealed to him precise ways He was answering this prayer.[2]

One mother chose this verse to pray for her daughter and her husband when they married: "I pray 'that your love may abound more and more in knowledge and depth of insight so that you may be able to discern what is best and may be pure and blameless until the day of Christ, filled with the fruit of righteousness that comes through Jesus Christ—to the glory and praise of God'" (Phil. 1:9-11).

Our prayers for our children should include promises God has made regarding children. We also can include requests made by other parents in the Bible. To form your own prayer for your children, find verses that give promises to parents or that indicate His will regarding children.

Using Paul's Words

We're approaching holy ground when we listen to someone who is in earnest prayer. Yet Paul invites us to do just that. On the surface, we might think Paul's prayers are rather general and wouldn't apply to those for whom we pray. On the contrary, Paul requested exactly what produces spiritual maturity. Who of us wouldn't want someone to pray that we'll be strengthened by His Spirit so Christ may dwell in our hearts through faith? (Eph. 3:16-19). Frequently he requested that they grow in spiritual wisdom and understanding. Reflection upon Paul's requests enables us to see how shallow our requests often are.

I've found it to be a great help to memorize Paul's prayers in the first chapters of Ephesians, Philippians, and Colossians. As I've quoted them in prayer, I've been impressed that Paul's most frequent request for these people for whom he faithfully prayed was that they would grow in their knowledge of God. Paul had thought deeply about what brings spiritual growth.

Paul's prayers encourage me to offer requests I otherwise would not have considered. For instance, I noticed that he told the Corinthians that he prayed that they would "not do anything wrong. . . . Our prayer is for your perfection" (2 Cor. 13:7, 9).

Paul assures us in Phil. 4:19 that God will supply all our needs according to his glorious riches in Christ Jesus. It is appropriate that we turn such promises into confident petitions: *Meet all his [her] needs according to Your glorious riches in Christ Jesus.* Praying scripture increases our confidence.

You may want to make a list of scriptures you can turn into prayers, such as the following:

Help him [her] to be joyful always, pray continually, and to give thanks in all circumstances, recognizing that this is God's will for him [her] in Christ Jesus (1 Thess. 5:16-18).

Help him [her] never to tire of doing what is right (2 Thess. 3:13).

Help him [her] not to rely on himself [herself] but on God (2 Cor. 1:9).

Make all grace abound to him [her], so that in all things at all times, having all that he [she] needs, he [she] will abound in every good work (2 Cor. 9:8).

I pray that out of Your glorious riches, You would strengthen them with power through Your Spirit in their inner beings, so that Christ may dwell in their hearts through faith (Eph. 3:16-17).

How it must please the Lord to see our hearts hunger for the exact things He has promised to give! When we bring His promises to Him and wait in expectation, He will not fail to give us according to His written Word.

MEDITATION

God loves for us to pray using the words He inspired. Consider the power we have when we take the Sword of the Spirit—the Word of God—with us when we pray.

These Words Are Life

"The LORD is near to all who call on him, to all who call on him in truth" (Ps. 145:18).

"These are written that you may believe" (John 20:31).

"Faith comes from listening to this message of good news—the Good News about Christ" (Rom. 10:17, NLT).

"Take . . . the sword of the Spirit, which is the word of God. And pray in the Spirit on all occasions" (Eph. 6:17-18).

"Until heaven and earth disappear, not the smallest letter, not the least stroke of a pen, will by any means disappear from the Law until everything is accomplished" (Matt 5:18).

"I am watching to see that my word is fulfilled" (Jer. 1:12).

"Thou hast magnified thy word above all thy name" (Ps. 138:2, KJV).

"Not one word has failed of all the good promises he gave through his servant Moses" (1 Kings 8:56).

"The LORD is faithful to all his promises and loving toward all he has made" (Ps. 145:13).

What does the Spirit say to me through these words?

How will I respond?

Lord, teach me to turn Your Words into confident petitions.

13 Read with Understanding

THIS MORNING OUR DAUGHTER CALLED. "Guess what Peter is doing!" At age 15 months, our grandson does something new, worth reporting on, nearly every day. However, today's news was extra special. "He's feeding himself yogurt with a spoon." I, his proud grandma, was appropriately amazed. Before our conversation ended, however, Peter had turned the yogurt upside down, said "Uh-oh!" and began using his hands.

Could it be our Heavenly Father is proud of us when we begin to feed ourselves? At times, we may go at it clumsily, and more advanced scholars might laugh at our attempts, but I believe Jesus is cheering us on. He must love it when we discover how to feed on His Word. My favorite directions on how to effectively feed ourselves are Solomon's words in Prov. 2:1-5. Notice the action words in these lines:

My son, if you accept my words and store up my commands within you, turning your ear to wisdom and applying your heart to understanding, and if you call out for insight and cry aloud for understanding, and if you look for it as for silver and search for it as for hidden treasure, then you will understand the fear of the LORD and find the knowledge of God.

It seems that Solomon calls us to go beyond receiving and even memorizing the words to understanding them. When we understand scripture, we recognize how to obey it. In His story

of the farmer scattering seed, Jesus said that if we don't understand the Word, the evil one has access to it (Matt. 13:19). What
we fail to understand does not take root in our lives; it will make
no change in how we live. So just as Daniel set himself to gain
understanding (Dan. 10:12), we refuse to be content until we
have learned to apply what we read.

If we cry with David, "I long to obey your commandments!"
(Ps. 119:40, NLT), the Lord delights to give us understanding. At
times He may teach us through a friend as we meet together in
Bible studies. "As iron sharpens iron, so one man sharpens another" (Prov. 27:17). For further insights, we may ask a pastor or
other spiritual leader or read a commentary on the verse. We
search as eagerly for wisdom as we would for lost money.

Consult Various Versions

One of the most profitable ways to feed on the Word ourselves before consulting other resources is to compare different
translations and paraphrases. Often a word can be translated various ways, and each version may bring out a different aspect of
its meaning. There are dangers here, however, in that the trans-
lator, though honest, may write something that the original
writer did not intend to say. Their paraphrases may reflect the
preferences of the translator(s) rather than the exact meaning of
the original language.

I grew up reading the King James Version, translated in En-
gland in the 1600s during the reign of King James. When the
New International Version came out, I began reading this mod-
ern translation with some qualms. *Is this really what the verse
means?* I would wonder. I found I was immensely enjoying reading it, however, and understanding more when reading this less
archaic wording.

My skepticism began to vanish the day I read 2 Cor. 2:14—
"But thanks be to God, who always leads us in triumphal proces-
sion in Christ and through us spreads everywhere the fragrance

of the knowledge of Christ." God encouraged me through these words, and when I checked out this verse in the King James Version, I wasn't at all sure I would have understood the message: "Now thanks be unto God, which always causeth us to triumph in Christ, and maketh manifest the savour of his knowledge by us in every place." My hunger to hear from God helped me realize that if I could more easily hear His message in another version, I would read that version as long as it was generally considered reliable.

A few years ago we gave the *New Living Translation* to a friend for Christmas. Months later he remarked, "I used to just read one or two chapters. Now I read and read. It's so interesting." Sometimes a new translation will give a freshness and clarity to words we've read repeatedly.

If you're going to purchase only one Bible, I suggest you choose a translation—rather than a paraphrase, such as *The Message* or *The Living Bible.* Translations are generally considered to be closer to the original texts, while paraphrases often rephrase rather freely. A paraphrase is not an accurate translation of the Bible nor is it promoted as such. My mother liked to have *The Living Bible* (paraphrased by Kenneth Taylor) available to use as a commentary. "How did Kenneth Taylor say that?" she would question while reading her King James Version. *The Living Bible* would often simplify a rather complex King James Version rendering. Taylor himself suggests, "For study purposes, a paraphrase should be checked against a rigid translation."

When a word is translated from the Hebrew or Aramaic (Old Testament) or Greek (New Testament), often it has a wide range of meanings. Most translations choose one of those meanings. The *Amplified Bible,* true to its name, amplifies the sentences by giving various meanings of key words. Reading the *Amplified Bible* lists of possible meanings for each word is at times rather cumbersome, but this version may well be helpful as a second Bible.

Compare 1 Pet. 5:7 in these various versions, and you'll understand why having more than one version can be a bonus.[1]

King James Version (reading grade level: 12)—"Casting all your care upon him; for he careth for you."

New King James Version (reading grade level: 9)—"Casting all your care upon Him, for he cares for you."

New International Version (reading grade level: 7.80)—"Cast all your anxiety on him because he cares for you."

New American Standard Bible, considered by some scholars to be the most true to the original (reading grade level: 9)— "Casting all your anxiety upon Him, because He cares for you."

New Living Translation (reading grade level: 6.30)—"Give all your worries and cares to God, for he cares about what happens to you."

The *Amplified Bible* (reading grade level: not available)— "Casting the whole of your care [all your anxieties, all your worries, all your concerns, once and for all] on Him; for He cares for you affectionately and cares about you watchfully."

The Living Bible, a paraphrase (reading grade level: 6.30)— "Let him have all your worries and cares, for he is always thinking about you and watching everything that concerns you."

The Message, a paraphrase (reading grade level: 5)—"Live carefree before God; he is most careful with you."

Also available is the *New International Readers Version*, a simplified version of the NIV, intended for children or readers for whom English is a second language. (Reading grade level 3.)

Read and Read Again

Four-year-old Amy, who lived next door, stood in our family room looking at a stack of Bibles. "You have a lot of Bibles in your house, so you know all about God," she declared matter-of-factly. Having a stack of Bibles may help, but more important is having some study methods in place. A few study books help too.

Sometimes our most profitable study will simply be reading

and rereading the Scripture text. Not many of us will match the effort G. Campbell Morgan gave to this method.

Years ago when John G. Mitchell, founder of Multnomah School of the Bible, had the opportunity to sit down with G. Campbell Morgan, called "the prince of Bible expositors," he had a question ready for him: "Dr. Morgan, tell me how you study your Bible."

Morgan just looked at him. Finally he said, "Mitchell, you wouldn't do it if I told you."

"Well," said Mitchell, "you try me."

He paused a moment and then said, "Before I study a book in the Bible, I read it through forty or fifty times—before I even start to study it."

Now we understand why G. Campbell Morgan's commentaries are filled with rich insights. He writes, "Read the book; read it again. Then read it again and yet again, until you become conscious that the book has made an impression upon your mind; that you have a conception of its general movement."[2]

If you read an entire book without stopping, it begins to open up. Fascinating ideas running through the book appear. Tim La-Haye in his book *How to Study the Bible for Yourself* suggests reading an entire book of the Bible every day for 30 days. (This method works best for books containing six chapters or less.) By the 30th day you will really know that particular book of the Bible. He adds that this method should probably not be used until you have read through the entire New Testament at least once.[3]

The best commentary on a verse is the Bible itself. In other words, the best way to understand what a verse means is to see what other passages say on the same topic. While you read, you may encounter a word that you want to understand more fully, so you will want to have access to a concordance. A concordance will guide you to other passages that contain a particular word. Choose some prominent word from the passage you are studying, and look it up in a concordance. Sometimes the references in the margin of your Bible give similar help, but the choice of passages will be fewer than in a concordance.

The Exhaustive Concordance of the Bible, by J. Strong and based on the King James Version, is available as a book or software. Internet sites such as crosswalk.com also provide a concordance online, giving you the ability to look up single words or phrases. Use your concordance to help study Bible characters or to learn the meaning of proper names. Every name in the Bible, especially Hebrew names, has a unique meaning and often gives insight into God's purposes.

To do a topical study on such topics as grace, prayer, or love, a helpful book is the *Beacon Dictionary of Theology*, edited by Richard S. Taylor and Kenneth Grider.

To read a clear, concise overview of every book of the Bible, purchase the fascinating book *What the Bible Is All About*, by Henrietta C. Mears. Other books to assist you in learning to study include *How to Read the Bible for All It's Worth*, by Gordon Fee and Douglas Stuart, and *Understanding Scripture: How to Read and Study the Bible*, by A. Berkeley Mickelsen and Alvera M. Mickelsen.

Study books never take the place of reflective reading. Merely gaining intellectual understanding leaves us famished. No matter which way we approach the study of the Scriptures, our most satisfying feeding will generally be what the Spirit teaches us as we read, ponder, reflect, and listen with a heart that's hungry to know God.

MEDITATION

The point of study is to stir in you a greater love for God. As you read these verses, consider: *In what new ways can I immerse myself in God's Word?*

These Words Are Life

"When anyone hears the message about the kingdom and

does not understand it, the evil one comes and snatches away what was sown in his heart" (Matt. 13:19).

"As iron sharpens iron, so one man sharpens another" (Prov. 27:17).

"Now the Bereans were of more noble character than the Thessalonians, for they received the message with great eagerness and examined the Scriptures every day to see if what Paul said was true" (Acts 17:11).

"Do your best to present yourself to God as one approved, a workman who does not need to be ashamed and who correctly handles the word of truth" (2 Tim. 2:15).

"Since the day we heard about you, we have not stopped praying for you and asking God to fill you with the knowledge of his will through all spiritual wisdom and understanding" (Col. 1:9).

"My purpose is that . . . they may have the full riches of complete understanding, in order that they may know the mystery of God, namely, Christ" (Col. 2:2).

What does the Spirit teach me through these words?

How will I respond?

Lord, I want to apply my heart to understanding so I can discover "the depth of the riches of the wisdom and knowledge of God" (Rom. 11:33).

14 Establishing Your Routine

I PRAY THAT AS YOU'VE READ THE PAGES OF THIS BOOK, you've received the gift of desire. Cherish that gift. As you follow through with a small desire, God will reward you with more desire.

"One thing that helped me was asking God to increase my desire," one lady said. Then she added, "But whether you sense desire or not, just do it!" If you possessed a consuming hunger to hear God speak, you would plan your day around the encounter. Why not make that plan now?

• Decide the best time of day for you to listen. Allow at least 15 minutes. Soon you will often find 15 minutes to be much too brief.

• Settle on a place where you'll be relatively free of distractions.

• Find a notebook in which to record your treasures.

• Resolve to keep your appointment with God for the next 21 days—the length of time required to establish a new habit.

• Decide which book of the Bible you will read, or use the lectionary on the following pages.

• Listen attentively, going to God's Word with prayerful anticipation. "Speak, LORD, for your servant is listening" (1 Sam. 3:9). God will speak to you as freshly as He spoke to those who first wrote the Bible. His words are still alive. "They are not just idle words for you—they are your life" (Deut. 32:47). If you come anticipating an encounter with God and longing to obey what He says, your life will be changed.

As you take in His words, eager to live by them, God's Spirit accompanies those words. Oswald Smith said that to be filled with the Word is the same as being filled with the Spirit. It's fascinating to note that in Acts these two terms appear to describe a single concept. Peter stated that the Gentiles had "received the Holy Spirit" (10:47). A few verses later, he stated, "The Gentiles also had received the word of God" (11:1). When you receive God's Word into your life, you're welcoming His Holy Spirit. His Spirit will work through your obedience to transform your actions, attitudes, disposition, and priorities—your entire life.

God gives you a hunger to spend time alone with Him consistently because He has something to say to you—something that will change your life!

Consider the Lectionary

"I decided to read half the Bible for Lent," a friend said and then admitted that she had begun reading at the beginning but eventually lost interest.

She assumed, as many do, that we must begin reading the Bible where we begin other books—at the beginning. The Bible, however, is actually 63 books in one cover and contains almost a million words. For such a huge manuscript, we need a reading plan.

So what is the best system to read? There are many ways to read the Bible, but one of the most profitable methods I've found is to use the readings listed in the daily lectionary (which means selected Bible readings). The first thing I do nearly every morning is to open my lectionary and write down the readings for that day. Each day's reading begins with the Psalms, followed by short selections from the Old Testament, a Gospel, and an Epistle.

This plan has been around for centuries. Sixteenth-century Archbishop Thomas Cranmer put together a two-year arrangement of scriptural readings to encourage daily Bible reading. Since then, Christians around the world have used his system printed in the *Book of Common Prayer.* In addition, others have also developed lectionaries, such as the *Revised Common Lectionary*, a three-year cycle that provides Sunday readings.

Using the lectionary gives an additional advantage beyond providing an answer to the question "Where shall I read?" The lectionary follows the church calendar, so at Christmastime we read about Jesus' birth. At Easter we read about His resurrection. Such readings help us prepare ourselves so we don't miss the spiritual value of religious holidays.

Some days you may find that you don't get through all the suggested passages. A young man told me recently that he had spent two hours on three verses by typing pages of thoughts he gained as he meditated. I suspect God is more pleased with such meditative reading than He is by our reading the entire day's selection with little reflection. We draw His attention by our humble and respectful approach to His Word. "This is the one I esteem: he who is humble and contrite in spirit, and trembles at my word" (Isa. 66:2).

Following the lectionary is only one profitable method of Bible reading. Other times you will want to read each book of the Bible in its entirety. But if you're new to Bible reading or you're not reading systematically through the Bible, I encourage you to use the lectionary.

MEDITATION

Allow these verses to encourage you to make your time alone with God the one thing you refuse to neglect.

These Words Are Life

"Wisdom is supreme; therefore get wisdom. Though it cost all you have, get understanding" (Prov. 4:7).

"You must commit yourselves wholeheartedly to these commands I am giving you today. Repeat them again and again to your children. Talk about them when you are at home and when you are away on a journey, when you are lying down and when you are getting up again" (Deut. 6:6-7, NLT).

"I am overwhelmed continually with a desire for your laws" (Ps. 119:20, NLT).

"[My determined purpose is] that I may know Him. . . . One thing I do" (Phil. 3:10, 13, AMP.)

"One thing have I desired of the LORD, that will I seek after; that I may dwell in the house of the LORD all the days of my life, to behold the beauty of the LORD, and to inquire in his temple" (Ps. 27:4, KJV).

What does the Spirit teach me through these words?

How will I respond?

Lord, strengthen my resolve to come regularly to Your Word. Remind me that the days I am inclined to omit Bible reading may be the days that my faithfulness would be most blessed by You.

If you've made a decision to spend time with God's Word or if your love for His Word is renewed, I would love to hear from you. You can write to me at Women Alive, P.O. Box 480052, Kansas City, MO 64148, or E-mail me by going to <www.womenalivemagazine.org> and contacting the editor.

The Daily Lectionary

THE DAILY LECTIONARY IS ARRANGED IN A TWO-YEAR CYCLE that will move you through most of the Bible in two years. The church year and the lectionary readings both begin with Advent in November and December.

Begin reading in Year One if the first Sunday of Advent is in an even-numbered year. For example, when the First Sunday of Advent is in November 2004, the lectionary for Year One is begun so most of Year One will be read in 2005. Most of Year Two will be read in even-numbered years.

The Psalms are listed first. Both morning and evening readings are given, but these may all be read in the morning.

The lectionary on the following pages is a slightly revised version of that arranged by Archbishop Thomas Cranmer in the 1500s. For instance, additional readings have been added to Christmas and Easter. Many of the optional passages were omitted simplifying the listing.

An exact date is not given for some of the weeks, because the lectionary follows the church calendar, and the dates vary from year to year. When necessary, use your monthly calendar to count the weeks from Easter or Christmas.

YEAR ONE
(Start in even-numbered years)

	Psalm	Old Testament	Epistle	Gospel
Week 1 Advent (Four Sundays before Christmas)				
S	A.M. 146, 147 P.M. 111, 112, 113	Isa. 1:1-9	2 Pet. 3:1-10	Matt. 25:1-13
M	A.M. 1, 2, 3 P.M. 4, 7	Isa. 1:10-20	1 Thess. 1:1-10	Luke 20:1-8
T	A.M. 5, 6 P.M. 10, 11	Isa. 1:21-31	1 Thess. 2:1-12	Luke 20:9-18
W	A.M. 119:1-24 P.M. 12, 13, 14	Isa. 2:1-11	1 Thess. 2:13-20	Luke 20:19-26
T	A.M. 18:1-20 P.M. 18:21-50	Isa. 2:12-22	1 Thess. 3:1-13	Luke 20:27-40
F	A.M. 16, 17 P.M. 22	Isa. 3:8-15	1 Thess. 4:1-12	Luke 20:41—21:4

	Psalm	Old Testament	Epistle	Gospel
S	A.M. 20, 21:1-7 P.M. 110:1-5, 116, 117	Isa. 4:2-6	1 Thess. 4:13-18	Luke 21:5-19

Week 2 Advent

	Psalm	Old Testament	Epistle	Gospel
S	A.M. 148, 149, 150 P.M. 114, 115	Isa. 5:1-7	2 Pet. 3:11-18	Luke 7:28-35
M	A.M. 25 P.M. 9, 15	Isa. 5:8-12, 18-23	1 Thess. 5:1-11	Luke 21:20-28
T	A.M. 26, 28 P.M. 36, 39	Isa. 5:13-17, 24-25	1 Thess. 5:12-28	Luke 21:29-38
W	A.M. 38 P.M. 119:25-48	Isa. 6:1-13	2 Thess. 1:1-12	John 7:53—8:11
T	A.M. 37:1-18 P.M. 37:19-42	Isa. 7:1-9	2 Thess. 2:1-12	Luke 22:1-13
F	A.M. 31 P.M. 35	Isa. 7:10-25	2 Thess. 2:13—3:5	Luke 22:14-30
S	A.M. 30, 32 P.M. 42, 43	Isa. 8:1-15	2 Thess. 3:6-18	Luke 22:31-38

Week 3 Advent

	Psalm	Old Testament	Epistle	Gospel
S	A.M. 63:1-8, 98 P.M. 103	Isa. 13:6-13	Heb. 12:18-29	John 3:22-30
M	A.M. 41, 52 P.M. 44	Isa. 8:16—9:1	2 Pet. 1:1-11	Luke 22:39-53
T	A.M. 45 P.M. 44	Isa. 9:1-7	2 Pet. 1:12-21	Luke 22:54-69
W	A.M. 119:49-72 P.M. 49	Isa. 9:8-17	2 Pet. 2:1-10	Mark 1:1-8
T	A.M. 50 P.M. 33	Isa. 9:18—10:4	2 Pet. 2:10-16	Matt. 3:1-12
F	A.M. 40, 54 P.M. 51	Isa. 10:5-19	2 Pet. 2:17-22	Matt. 11:2-15
S	A.M. 55 P.M. 138, 139:1-17	Isa. 10:20-27	Jude 17-25	Luke 3:19

Week 4 Advent

	Psalm	Old Testament	Epistle	Gospel
S	A.M. 24, 29 P.M. 8, 84	Isa. 42:1-12	Eph. 6:10-20	John 3:16-21
M	A.M. 61, 62 P.M. 112,115	Isa. 11:1-9	Rev. 20:1-10	John 5:30-47
T	A.M. 66, 67 P.M. 116, 117	Isa. 11:10-16	Rev. 20:11—21:8	Luke 1:5-25
W	A.M. 72 P.M. 111, 113	Isa. 28:9-22	Rev. 21:9-21	Luke 1:26-38
T	A.M. 80 P.M. 146, 147	Isa. 29:13-24	Rev. 21:22—22:5	Luke 1:39-48
F	A.M. 93, 96 P.M. 148, 150	Isa. 33:17-22	Rev. 22:6-11, 18-20	Luke 1:57-66

Dec. 24

	Psalm	Old Testament	Epistle	Gospel
	A.M. 45, 46	Isa. 35:1-10	Rev. 22:12-17, 21	Luke 1:67-80

Psalm	Old Testament	Epistle	Gospel
Christmas Eve			
A.M. 89:1-29	Isa. 59:15-21	Phil. 2:5-11	
Christmas Day and Following			
Christmas Day			
A.M. 2, 85 P.M. 110:1-1, 132	Zech. 2:10-13	1 John 4:7-16	John 3:31-26, Luke 2:1-20
First Sunday after Christmas			
A.M. 93, 96 P.M. 34	Isa. 62:6-7, 10-12	Heb 2:10-18	Matt. 1:18-25
Dec. 29			
A.M. 18:1-20 P.M. 18:21-50	Isa. 12:1-6	Rev. 1:1-8	John 7:37-52
Dec. 30			
A.M. 20, 21:1-7 P.M. 23, 27	Isa 25:1-9	Rev. 1:9-20	John 7:53—8:11
Dec. 31			
A.M. 46, 48	Isa. 26:1-9	2 Cor. 5:16—6:2	John 8:12-19
Eve of Holy Name			
A.M. 90	Isa. 65:15-25	Rev. 21:1-6	
Holy Name			
A.M. 103 P.M. 148	Gen. 17:1-12, 15-16	Col. 2:6-12	John 16:23-30
Second Sunday after Christmas			
A.M. 66, 67 P.M. 145	Jer. 31:7-14	1 John 2:12-17	John 6:41-47
Jan. 2			
A.M. 34 P.M. 33	Gen. 12:1-7	Heb. 11:1-12	John 6:35-42, 48-51
Jan. 3			
A.M. 68 P.M. 72	Gen. 28:10-22	Heb. 11:13-22	John 10:7-17
Jan. 4			
A.M. 85, 87 P.M. 89:1-29	Exod. 3:1-12	Heb. 11:23-31	John 14:6-14
Jan. 5			
A.M. 2, 110:1-5	Josh. 1:1-9	Heb. 11:32—12:2	John 15:1-16
Eve of Epiphany			
A.M. 29, 98	Isa. 66:18-23	Rom. 15:7-13	

The Epiphany
(Begins on January 6 and lasts until Lent)

Psalm	Old Testament	Epistle	Gospel
Epiphany			
A.M. 46, 97 P.M. 96, 100	Isa. 52:7-10	Rev. 21:22-27	Matt. 12:14-21

	Psalm	Old Testament	Epistle	Gospel
Jan. 7				
	A.M. 103 P.M. 114, 115	Isa. 52:3-6	Rev. 2:1-7	John 2:1-11
Jan. 8				
	A.M. 117, 118 P.M. 112, 113	Isa. 59:15-21	Rev. 2:8-17	John 4:46-54
Jan. 9				
	A.M. 121, 122, 123 P.M. 131, 132	Isa. 63:1-5	Rev. 2:18-29	John 5:1-15
Jan. 10				
	A.M. 138, 139:1-17 P.M. 147	Isa. 65:1-9	Rev. 3:1-6	John 6:1-14
Jan. 11				
	A.M. 148, 150 P.M. 91, 92	Isa. 65:13-16	Rev. 3:7-13	John 6:15-27
Jan. 12				
	A.M. 98, 99, 100	Isa. 66:1-2, 22-23	Rev. 3:14-22	John 9:1-12, 35-38
Eve of 1 Epiphany				
	A.M. 104	Isa. 61:1-9	Gal. 3:23-29, 4:4-7	
Week 1 Epiphany				
S	A.M. 146, 147 P.M. 111, 112, 113	Isa. 40:1-11	Heb. 1:1-12	John 1:1-7, 19-20, 29-34
M	A.M. 1, 2, 3 P.M. 4, 7	Isa. 40:12-23	Eph. 1:1-14	Mark 1:1-13
T	A.M. 5, 6 P.M. 10, 11	Isa. 40:25-31	Eph. 1:15-23	Mark 1:14-28
W	A.M. 119:1-24 P.M. 12, 13, 14	Isa. 41:1-16	Eph. 2:1-10	Mark 1:29-45
T	A.M. 18:1-20 P.M. 18:21-50	Isa. 41:17-29	Eph. 2:11-22	Mark 2:1-12
F	A.M. 16, 17 P.M. 22	Isa. 42:1-17	Eph. 3:1-13	Mark 2:13-22
S	A.M. 20, 21:1-7 P.M. 110:1-5, 116, 117	Isa. 43:1-13	Eph. 3:14-21	Mark 2:23—3:6
Week of 2 Epiphany				
S	A.M. 148, 149, 150 P.M. 114, 115	Isa. 43:14—44:5	Heb. 6:17—7:10	John 4:27-42
M	A.M. 25 P.M. 9, 15	Isa. 44:6-8, 21-23	Eph. 4:1-16	Mark 3:7-19
T	A.M. 26, 28 P.M. 36, 39	Isa. 44:9-20	Eph. 4:17-32	Mark 3:19-35
W	A.M. 38 P.M. 119:25-48	Isa. 44:24—45:7	Eph. 5:1-14	Mark 4:1-20
T	A.M. 37:1-18 P.M. 37:19-42	Isa. 45:5-17	Eph. 5:15-33	Mark 4:21-34
F	A.M. 31 P.M. 35	Isa. 45:18-25	Eph. 6:1-9	Mark 4:35-41

	Psalm	Old Testament	Epistle	Gospel
S	A.M. 30, 32 P.M. 42, 43	Isa. 46:1-13	Eph. 6:10-24	Mark 5:1-20

Week 3 Epiphany

	Psalm	Old Testament	Epistle	Gospel
S	A.M. 63:1-8, 98 P.M. 103	Isa. 47:1-15	Heb. 10:19-31	John 5:2-18
M	A.M. 41, 52 P.M. 44	Isa. 48:1-11	Gal. 1:1-17	Mark 5:21-43
T	A.M. 45 P.M. 47, 48	Isa. 48:12-21	Gal. 1:18—2:10	Mark 6:1-13
W	A.M. 119:49-72 P.M. 49	Isa. 49:1-12	Gal. 2:11-21	Mark 6:13-29
T	A.M. 50 P.M. 118	Isa. 49:13-23	Gal. 3:1-14	Mark 6:30-46
F	A.M. 40, 54 P.M. 51	Isa. 50:1-11	Gal. 3:15-22	Mark 6:47-56
S	A.M. 55 P.M. 138, 139:1-17	Isa. 51:1-8	Gal. 3:23-29	Mark 7:1-23

Week 4 Epiphany

	Psalm	Old Testament	Epistle	Gospel
S	A.M. 24, 29 P.M. 8, 84	Isa. 51:9-16	Heb. 11:8-16	John 7:14-31
M	A.M. 56, 57 P.M. 64, 65	Isa. 51:17-23	Gal. 4:1-11	Mark 7:24-37
T	A.M. 61, 62 P.M. 68:1-20, 24-36	Isa. 52:1-12	Gal. 4:12-20	Mark 8:1-10
W	A.M. 72 P.M. 119:73-96	Isa. 54:1-10	Gal. 4:21-31	Mark 8:11-26
T	A.M. 71 P.M. 74	Isa. 55:1-13	Gal. 5:1-15	Mark 8:27—9:1
F	A.M. 69:1-23, 31-38 P.M. 73	Isa. 56:1-8	Gal. 5:16-24	Mark 9:2-13
S	A.M. 75, 76 P.M. 23, 27	Isa. 57:3-13	Gal. 5:25—6:10	Mark 9:14-29

Week 5 Epiphany

	Psalm	Old Testament	Epistle	Gospel
S	A.M. 93, 96 P.M. 34	Isa. 57:14-21	Heb. 12:1-6	John 7:37-46
M	A.M. 80 P.M. 77	Isa. 58:1-12	Gal. 6:11-18	Mark 9:30-41
T	A.M. 78:1-39 P.M. 78:40-72	Isa. 59:1-15	2 Tim. 1:1-14	Mark 9:42-50
W	A.M. 119:97-120 P.M. 81, 82	Isa. 59:15-21	2 Tim. 1:15—2:13	Mark 10:1-16
T	A.M. 146, 147 P.M. 85, 86	Isa. 60:1-17	2 Tim. 2:14-26	Mark 10:17-31
F	A.M. 88 P.M. 91, 92	Isa. 61:1-9	2 Tim. 3:1-17	Mark 10:32-45
S	A.M. 87, 90 P.M. 136	Isa. 61:10—62:5	2 Tim. 4:1-8	Mark 10:46-52

	Psalm	Old Testament	Epistle	Gospel
Week 6 Epiphany				
S	A.M. 66, 67 P.M. 19, 46	Isa. 62:6-12	1 John 2:3-11	John 8:12-19
M	A.M. 89:1-18 P.M. 89:19-52	Isa. 63:1-6	1 Tim. 1:1-17	Mark 11:1-11
T	A.M. 97, 99 P.M. 94	Isa. 63:7-14	1 Tim. 1:18—2:8	Mark 11:12-26
W	A.M. 101, 109:1-4, 20-30 P.M. 119:121-144	Isa 63:15—64:9	1 Tim. 3:1-16	Mark 11:27—12:12
T	A.M. 105:1-22 P.M. 105:23-45	Isa. 65:1-12	1 Tim. 4:1-16	Mark 12:13-27
F	A.M. 102 P.M. 107:1-32	Isa. 65:17-25	1 Tim. 5:17-22	Mark 12:28-34
S	A.M. 107:33-43, 108:1-6 P.M. 33	Isa. 66:1-6	1 Tim. 6:6-21	Mark 12:35-44
Week 7 Epiphany				
S	A.M. 118 P.M. 145	Isa. 66:7-14	1 John 3:4-10	John 10:7-16
M	A.M. 106:1-18 P.M. 106:19-48	Ruth 1:1-14	2 Cor. 1:1-11	Matt. 5:1-12
T	A.M. 121, 122, 123 P.M. 124, 125, 126	Ruth 1:15-22	2 Cor. 1:12-22	Matt. 5:13-20
W	A.M. 119:145-176 P.M. 128, 129, 130	Ruth 2:1-13	2 Cor. 1:23—2:17	Matt. 5:21-26
T	A.M. 131, 132 P.M. 134, 135	Ruth 2:14-23	2 Cor. 3:1-18	Matt. 5:27-37
F	A.M. 140, 142 P.M. 141, 143:1-11	Ruth 3:1-18	2 Cor. 4:1-12	Matt. 5:38-48
S	A.M. 137:1-7, 144 P.M. 104	Ruth 4:1-17	2 Cor. 4:13—5:10	Matt. 6:1-16
Week 8 Epiphany				
S	A.M. 146, 147 P.M. 111, 112, 113	Deut. 4:1-9	2 Tim. 4:1-8	John 12:1-8
M	A.M. 1, 2, 3 P.M. 4, 7	Deut. 4:9-14	2 Cor. 10:1-18	Matt. 6:7-15
T	A.M. 5, 6 P.M. 10, 11	Deut. 4:15-24	2 Cor. 11:1-21	Matt. 6:16-23
W	A.M. 119:1-24 P.M. 12, 13, 14	Deut. 4:25-31	2 Cor. 11:21-33	Matt. 6:24-34
T	A.M. 18:1-20 P.M. 18:21-50	Deut. 4:32-40	2 Cor. 12:1-10	Matt. 7:1-12
F	A.M. 16, 17 P.M. 22	Deut. 5:1-22	2 Cor. 12:11-21	Matt. 7:13-21
S	A.M. 20, 21:1-7 P.M. 110:1-5, 116, 117	Deut. 5:22-33	2 Cor. 13:1-14	Matt. 7:22-29
Week of Last Epiphany				
S	A.M. 148, 149, 150 P.M. 114, 115	Deut. 6:1-9	Heb. 12:18-29	John 12:24-32

	Psalm	Old Testament	Epistle	Gospel
M	A.M. 25 P.M. 9, 15	Deut. 6:10-15	Heb. 1:1-14	John 1:1-18
T	A.M. 26, 28 P.M. 36, 39	Deut. 6:16-25	Heb. 2:1-10	John 1:19-28
Ash Wednesday				
	A.M. 95, 32, 143 P.M. 102, 130	Jon. 3:1—4:11	Heb. 12:1-14	Luke 18:9-14
T	A.M. 37:1-18 P.M. 37:19-42	Deut. 7:6-11	Titus 1:1-16	John 1:29-34
F	A.M. 95, 31 P.M. 35	Deut. 7:12-16	Titus 2:1-15	John 1:35-42
S	A.M. 30, 32 P.M. 42, 43	Deut. 7:17-26	Titus 3:1-15	John 1:43-51

Lent

Week 1 Lent (Begins on Wednesday seven weeks before Easter)

	Psalm	Old Testament	Epistle	Gospel
S	A.M. 63:1-8 98 P.M. 103	Deut. 8:1-10	1 Cor. 1:17-31	Mark 2:18-22
M	A.M. 41, 52 P.M. 44	Deut. 8:11-20	Heb. 2:11-18	John 2:1-12
T	A.M. 45 P.M. 47, 48	Deut. 9:4-12	Heb. 3:1-11	John 2:13-22
W	A.M. 119:49-72 P.M. 49	Deut. 9:13-21	Heb. 3:12-19	John 2:23—3:15
T	A.M. 50 P.M. 19, 46	Deut. 9:23—10:5	Heb. 4:1-10	John 3:16-21
F	A.M. 95, 40, 54 P.M. 51	Deut. 10:12-22	Heb. 4:11-16	John 3:22-36
S	A.M. 55 P.M. 138, 139:1-17	Deut. 11:18-28	Heb. 5:1-10	John 4:1-26

Week 2 Lent

	Psalm	Old Testament	Epistle	Gospel
S	A.M. 24, 29 P.M. 8, 84	Jer. 1:1-10	1 Cor. 3:11-23	Mark 3:31—4:9
M	A.M. 56, 57 P.M. 64, 65	Jer. 1:11-19	Rom. 1:1-15	John 4:27-42
T	A.M. 61, 62 P.M. 68:1-20, 24-36	Jer. 2:1-13	Rom. 1:16-25	John 4:43-54
W	A.M. 72 P.M. 119:73-96	Jer. 3:6-18	Rom. 1:28—2:11	John 5:1-18
T	A.M. 71 P.M. 74	Jer. 4:9-10, 19-28	Rom. 2:12-24	John 5:19-29
F	A.M. 95, 69:1-23, 31-38 P.M. 73	Jer. 5:1-9	Rom. 2:25—3:18	John 5:30-47
S	A.M. 75, 76 P.M. 23, 27	Jer. 5:20-31	Rom. 3:19-31	John 7:1-13

Week 3 Lent

	Psalm	Old Testament	Epistle	Gospel
S	A.M. 93, 96 P.M. 34	Jer. 6:9-15	1 Cor. 6:12-20	Mark 5:1-20

	Psalm	Old Testament	Epistle	Gospel
M	A.M. 80 P.M. 77	Jer. 7:1-15	Rom. 4:1-12	John 7:14-36
T	A.M. 78:1-39 P.M. 78:40-72	Jer. 7:21-34	Rom. 4:13-25	John 7:37-52
W	A.M. 119:97-120 P.M. 81, 82	Jer. 8:18—9:6	Rom. 5:1-11	John 8:12-20
T	A.M. 42, 43 P.M. 85, 86	Jer. 10:11-24	Rom. 5:12-21	John 8:21-32
F	A.M. 95, 88 P.M. 91, 92	Jer. 11:1-8, 14-20	Rom. 6:1-11	John 8:33-47
S	A.M. 87, 90 P.M. 136	Jer. 13:1-11	Rom. 6:12-23	John 8:47-59

Week 4 Lent

	Psalm	Old Testament	Epistle	Gospel
S	A.M. 66, 67 P.M. 19, 46	Jer. 14:1-9, 17-22	Gal. 4:21—5:1	Mark 8:11-21
M	A.M. 89:1-18 P.M. 89:19-52	Jer. 16:10-21	Rom. 7:1-12	John 6:1-15
T	A.M. 97, 99 P.M. 94	Jer. 17:19-27	Rom. 7:13-25	John 6:16-27
W	A.M. 101, 109:1-4, 20-30 P.M. 119:121-144	Jer. 18:1-11	Rom. 8:1-11	John 6:27-40
T	A.M. 69:1-23, 31-38 P.M. 73	Jer. 22:13-23	Rom. 8:12-27	John 6:41-51
F	A.M. 95, 102 P.M. 107:1-32	Jer. 23:1-8	Rom. 8:28-39	John 6:52-59
S	A.M. 107:33-43, 108:1-6 P.M. 33	Jer. 23:9-15	Rom. 9:1-18	John 6:60-71

Week 5 Lent

	Psalm	Old Testament	Epistle	Gospel
S	A.M. 118 P.M. 145	Jer. 23:16-32	1 Cor. 9:19-27	Mark 8:31—9:1
M	A.M. 31 P.M. 35	Jer. 24:1-10	Rom. 9:19-23	John 9:1-17
T	A.M. 121, 122, 123 P.M. 124, 125, 126	Jer. 25:8-17	Rom. 10:1-13	John 9:18-41
W	A.M. 119:145-176 P.M. 128, 129, 130	Jer. 25:30-38	Rom. 10:14-21	John 10:1-18
T	A.M. 131, 132 P.M. 140, 142	Jer. 26:1-16	Rom. 11:1-12	John 10:19-42
F	A.M. 95, 22 P.M. 141, 143:1-11	Jer. 29:1, 4-13	Rom. 11:13-24	John 11:1-27
S	A.M. 137:1-6, 144 P.M. 42, 43	Jer. 31:27-34	Rom. 11:25-36	John 11:28-44

Holy Week

Palm Sunday

	Psalm	Old Testament	Epistle	Gospel
	A.M. 24, 29 P.M. 103	Zech. 9:9-12	1 Tim. 6:12-16	Matt. 21:12-17
M	A.M. 51:1-18 P.M. 69:1-23	Jer. 12:1-16	Phil. 3:1-14	John 12:9-19

	Psalm	Old Testament	Epistle	Gospel
T	A.M. 6, 12 P.M. 94	Jer. 15:10-21	Phil. 3:15-21	John 12:20-26
W	A.M. 55 P.M. 74	Jer. 17:5-10, 14-17	Phil. 4:1-13	John 12:27-26
Maundy Thursday				
	A.M. 102 P.M. 142, 143	Jer. 20:7-11	1 Cor. 10:14-17, 11:27-32	John 17:1-11
Good Friday				
	A.M. 95, 22 P.M. 40:1-14, 54	Gen. 22:1-14	1 Peter 1:10-20	John 13:36-38, 19:38-42
Holy Saturday				
	A.M. 88 P.M. 27	Job 19:21-27	Heb. 4:1-16	Rom. 8:1-11

Easter Week

	Psalm	Old Testament	Epistle	Gospel
Easter Day				
	A.M. 148, 149, 150 P.M. 113, 114	Exod. 12:1-14	Isa. 51:9-11	John 1:1-18, 20:1-23 Luke 24:13-35
M	A.M. 93, 98 P.M. 66	Jon. 2:1-9	Acts 2:14, 22-32	John 14:1-14
T	A.M. 103 P.M. 111, 114	Isa. 30:18-21	Acts 2:26-41	John 14:15-31
W	A.M. 97, 99 P.M. 115	Mic. 7:7-15	Acts 3:1-10	John 15:1-11
T	A.M. 146, 147 P.M. 148, 149	Ezek. 37:1-14	Acts 3:11-26	John 15:12-27
F	A.M. 136 P.M. 118	Dan. 12:1-4, 13	Acts 4:1-12	John 16:1-15
S	A.M. 145 P.M. 104	Isa. 25:1-9	Acts 4:13-21	John 16:16-33

Week 2 Easter

	Psalm	Old Testament	Epistle	Gospel
S	A.M. 146, 147 P.M. 111, 112, 113	Isa. 43:8-13	1 Pet. 2:2-10	John 14:1-7
M	A.M. 1, 2, 3 P.M. 4, 7	Dan. 1:1-21	1 John 1:1-10	John 17:1-11
T	A.M. 5, 6 P.M. 10, 11	Dan. 2:1-16	1 John 2:1-11	John 17:12-19
W	A.M. 119:1-24 P.M. 12, 13, 14	Dan. 2:17-30	1 John 2:12-17	John 17:20-26
T	A.M. 18:1-20 P.M. 18:21-50	Dan. 2:31-49	1 John 2:18-29	Luke 3:1-14
F	A.M. 16, 17 P.M. 134, 135	Dan. 3:1-18	1 John 3:1-10	Luke 3:15-22
S	A.M. 20, 21:1-7 P.M. 110:1-5, 116, 117	Dan. 3:19-30	1 John 3:11-18	Luke 4:1-13

Week 3 Easter

	Psalm	Old Testament	Epistle	Gospel
S	A.M. 148, 149, 150 P.M. 114, 115	Dan. 4:1-18	1 Pet. 4:7-11	John 21:15-25

	Psalm	Old Testament	Epistle	Gospel
M	A.M. 25 P.M. 9, 15	Dan. 4:19-27	1 John 3:19—4:6	Luke 4:14-30
T	A.M. 26, 28 P.M. 36, 39	Dan. 4:28-37	1 John 4:7-21	Luke 4:31-37
W	A.M. 38 P.M. 119:25-48	Dan. 5:1-12	1 John 5:1-12	Luke 4:38-44
W	A.M. 37:1-18 P.M. 37:19-42	Dan. 5:13-30	1 John 5:13-20	Luke 5:1-11
F	A.M. 105:1-22 P.M. 105:23-45	Dan. 6:1-15	2 John 1-13	Luke 5:12-26
S	A.M. 30, 32 P.M. 42, 43	Dan. 6:16-28	3 John 1-15	Luke 5:27-39

Week 4 Easter

	Psalm	Old Testament	Epistle	Gospel
S	A.M. 63:1-8, 98 P.M. 103	Exod. 14:10-18	1 Pet. 5:1-11	Matt. 7:15-29
M	A.M. 41, 52 P.M. 44	Exod. 14:10-31	Col. 1:1-14	Luke 6:1-11
T	A.M. 45 P.M. 47, 48	Exod. 15:1-13	Col. 1:15-23	Luke 6:12-26
W	A.M. 119:49-72 P.M. 49	Exod. 19:1-9, 16-20	Col. 1:24—2:7	Luke 6:27-38
T	A.M. 50 P.M. 114, 115	Neh. 9:6-15	Col. 2:8-23	Luke 6:39-49
F	A.M. 40, 54 P.M. 51	Dan. 7:9-14	Col. 3:1-11	Luke 7:1-17
S	A.M. 55 P.M. 138, 139:1-17	Gen. 8:6-22	Col. 3:12-17	Luke 7:18-28, 31-35

Week 5 Easter

	Psalm	Old Testament	Epistle	Gospel
S	A.M. 24, 29 P.M. 8, 84	Isa. 49:8-18	2 Thess. 2:13-17	Matt. 7:7-14
M	A.M. 56, 57 P.M. 64, 65	Zech. 9:9-12	Col. 3:2-18	Luke 7:36-50
T	A.M. 61, 62 P.M. 68:1-20, 24-36	Isa. 42:1-9	Rom. 12:1-21	Luke 8:1-15
W	A.M. 72 P.M. 119:73-96	Isa. 45:21-25	Rom 13:1-14	Luke 8:16-25
T	A.M. 71 P.M. 74	Isa. 49:1-6	Rom. 14:1-12	Luke 8:26-39
F	A.M. 106:1-18 P.M. 106:19-48	Isa. 52:13—53:12	Rom. 14:13-23	Luke 8:40-56
S	A.M. 75, 76 P.M. 23, 27	Gen. 9:8-16	Rom. 15:1-13	Luke 9:1-17

Week 6 Easter

	Psalm	Old Testament	Epistle	Gospel
S	A.M. 93, 96 P.M. 34	Isa. 41:17-20	1 Tim. 3:14—4:5	Matt. 13:24-34
M	A.M. 80 P.M. 77	Deut. 8:1-10	James 1:1-15	Luke 9:18-27
T	A.M. 78:1-39 P.M. 78:40-72	Deut. 8:11-20	James 1:16-27	Luke 11:1-13

	Psalm	Old Testament	Epistle	Gospel
W	A.M. 119:97-120	Daniel 7:9-14	James 5:13-18	Luke 12:22-31
Eve of Ascension				
	A.M. 68:1-20	2 Kings 2:1-15	Rev. 5:1-14	
Ascension Day				
	A.M. 8, 47 P.M. 24, 96	Ezek. 1:1-14, 24-28	Heb. 2:5-18	Matt. 28:16-20
F	A.M. 85, 86 P.M. 91, 92	Ezek. 1:28—3:3	Heb. 4:14—5:6	Luke 9:28-36
S	A.M. 87, 90 P.M. 136	Ezek. 3:4-17	Heb. 5:7-14	Luke 9:37-50
Week 7 Easter				
S	A.M. 66, 67 P.M. 19, 46	Ezek. 3:16-27	Eph. 2:1-10	Matt. 10:24-33, 40-42
M	A.M. 89:1-18 P.M. 89:19-52	Ezek. 4:1-17	Heb. 6:1-12	Luke 9:51-62
T	A.M. 97, 99 P.M. 94	Ezek. 7:10-15, 23-27	Heb. 6:13-20	Luke 10:1-17
W	A.M. 101, 109:1-4, 20-30 P.M. 119:121-144	Ezek. 11:14-25	Heb. 7:1-17	Luke 10:17-24
T	A.M. 105:1-22 P.M. 105:23-45	Ezek. 18:1-4, 19-32	Heb. 7:18-28	Luke 10:25-37
F	A.M. 102 P.M. 107:1-32	Ezek. 34:17-31	Heb. 8:1-13	Luke 10:38-42
S	A.M. 107:33-43, 108:1-6	Ezek. 43:1-12	Heb. 9:1-14	Luke 11:14-23
Eve of Pentecost				
	A.M. 33	Exod. 19:3-8, 16-20	1 Pet. 2:4-10	
The Day of Pentecost				
	A.M. 118 P.M. 145	Isa. 11:1-9	1 Cor. 2:1-13	John 14:21-29
Eve of Trinity Sunday				
	A.M. 104	Gen. 11:1-9	Eph. 3:14-21	
Trinity Sunday				
	A.M. 146, 147 P.M. 111, 112, 113	Gen. 1:1-2:3	Eph. 4:1-16	John 1:1-18

The Season After Pentecost

The Season after Pentecost (called Ordinary Time) begins on the Monday after Pentecost and lasts until the day before the First Sunday in Advent.

Week 1				
M	A.M. 106:1-18 P.M. 106:19-48	Isa. 63:7-14	2 Tim. 1:1-14	Luke 11:24-36
T	A.M. 121, 122, 123 P.M. 124, 125, 126	Isa. 63:15—64:9	2 Tim. 1:15—2:13	Luke 11:37-52
W	A.M. 119:145-176 P.M. 128, 129, 130	Isa. 65:1-12	2 Tim. 2:14-26	Luke 11:53—12:12
T	A.M. 131, 132, P.M. 134, 135	Isa. 65:17-25	2 Tim. 3:1-17	Luke 12:13-31

	Psalm	Old Testament	Epistle	Gospel
F	A.M. 140, 142 P.M. 141, 143:1-11	Isa. 66:1-6	2 Tim. 4:1-8	Luke 12:32-48
S	A.M. 137:1-6, 144 P.M. 104	Isa. 66:7-14	2 Tim. 4:9-22	Luke 12:49-59

Week 2 (Week of the Sunday Closest to May 11)

	Psalm	Old Testament	Epistle	Gospel
S	A.M. 71:16-24	Lev. 19:1-2, 9-18	1 Cor. 3:10-11, 16-23	Matt. 5:38-48
M	A.M. 1, 2, 3 P.M. 4, 7	Ruth 1:1-18	1 Tim. 1:1-17	Luke 13:1-9
T	A.M. 5, 6 P.M. 10, 11	Ruth 1:19—2:13	1 Tim. 1:18-2:8	Luke 13:10-17
W	A.M. 119:1-24 P.M. 12, 13, 14	Ruth 2:14-23	1 Tim. 3:1-16	Luke 13:18-30
T	A.M. 18:1-20 P.M. 18:21-50	Ruth 3:1-18	1 Tim. 4:1-16	Luke 13:31-35
F	A.M. 16, 17 P.M. 22	Ruth 4:1-17	1 Tim. 5:17-22	Luke 14:1-11
S	A.M. 20, 21:1-7 P.M. 110:1-5, 116, 117	Deut. 1:1-8	1 Tim. 6:6-21	Luke 14:12-24

Week 3 (Week of the Sunday Closest to May 25)

	Psalm	Old Testament	Epistle	Gospel
S	A.M. 148, 149, 150 P.M. 114, 115	Deut. 4:1-9	Rev. 7:1-4, 9-17	Matt. 12:33-45
M	A.M. 25 P.M. 9, 15	Deut. 4:9-14	2 Cor. 1:1-11	Luke 14:25-35
T	A.M. 26, 28 P.M. 36, 39	Deut. 4:15-24	2 Cor. 1:12-22	Luke 15:1-10
W	A.M. 38 P.M. 119:25-48	Deut. 4:25-31	2 Cor. 1:23—2:17	Luke 15:1-2, 11-32
T	A.M. 37:1-18 P.M. 37:19-42	Deut. 4:32-40	2 Cor. 3:1-18	Luke 16:1-9
F	A.M. 31 P.M. 35	Deut. 5:1-22	2 Cor. 4:1-12	Luke 16:10-17
S	A.M. 30, 32 P.M. 42, 43	Deut. 5:22-33	2 Cor. 4:13—5:10	Luke 16:19-31

Week 4 (Week of the Sunday Closest to May 11)

	Psalm	Old Testament	Epistle	Gospel
S	A.M. 63:1-8, 98 P.M. 103	Deut. 11:1-12	Rev. 10:1-11	Matt. 13:44-58
M	A.M. 41, 52 P.M. 44	Deut. 11:13-19	2 Cor. 5:11—6:2	Luke 17:1-10
T	A.M. 45 P.M. 47, 48	Deut. 12:1-12	2 Cor. 6:3-13	Luke 17:11-19
W	A.M. 119:49-72 P.M. 49	Deut. 13:1-11	2 Cor. 7:2-16	Luke 17:20-37
T	A.M. 50 P.M. 8, 84	Deut. 16:18-20, 17:14-20	2 Cor. 8:1-16	Luke 18:1-8
F	A.M. 40, 54 P.M. 51	Deut. 26:1-11	2 Cor. 8:16-24	Luke 18:9-14
S	A.M. 55 P.M. 138, 139:1-17	Deut. 29:2-15	2 Cor. 9:1-15	Luke 18:15-30

	Psalm	Old Testament	Epistle	Gospel
Week 5 (Week of the Sunday Closest to June 8)				
S	A.M. 24, 29 P.M. 8, 84	Deut. 29:16-29	Rev. 12:1-12	Matt. 15:29-39
M	A.M. 56, 57 P.M. 64, 65	Deut. 30:1-10	2 Cor. 10:1-18	Luke 18:31-43
T	A.M. 61, 62 P.M. 68:1-20, 24-36	Deut. 30:11-20	2 Cor. 11:1-21	Luke 19:1-10
M	A.M. 72 P.M. 119:73-96	Deut. 31:30—32:14	2 Cor. 11:21-33	Luke 19:11-27
T	A.M. 71 P.M. 74	Hos. 5:15—6:6	2 Cor. 12:1-10	Luke 19:28-40
F	A.M. 69:1-23, 31-38 P.M. 73	Exod. 19:2-8	2 Cor. 12:11-21	Luke 19:41-48
S	A.M. 75, 76 P.M. 23, 27	1 Kings 3:5-12	2 Cor. 13:1-14	Luke 20:1-8
Week 6 (Week of the Sunday Closest to June 15)				
S	A.M. 93, 96 P.M. 34	Jer. 15:15-21	Rev. 15:1-8	Matt. 18:1-14
M	A.M. 80 P.M. 77	1 Sam. 1:1-20	Acts 1:1-14	Luke 20:9-19
T	A.M. 78:1-39 P.M. 78:40-72	1 Sam. 1:21—2:11	Acts 1:15-26	Luke 20:19-26
W	A.M. 119:97-120 P.M. 81, 82	1 Sam. 2:12-26	Acts 2:1-21	Luke 20:27-40
T	A.M. 34 P.M. 85, 86	1 Sam. 2:27-36	Acts 2:22-36	Luke 20:41—21:4
F	A.M. 88 P.M. 91, 92	1 Sam. 3:1-21	Acts 2:37-47	Luke 21:5-19
S	A.M. 87, 90 P.M. 136	1 Sam. 4:1-11	Acts 4:32—5:11	Luke 21:20-28
Week 7 (Week of the Sunday Closest to June 22)				
S	A.M. 66, 67 P.M. 19, 46	1 Sam. 4:12-22	James 1:1-18	Matt. 19:23-30
M	A.M. 89:1-18 P.M. 89:19-52	1 Sam. 5:1-12	Acts 5:12-26	Luke 21:29-36
T	A.M. 97, 99 P.M. 94	1 Sam. 6:1-16	Acts 5:27-42	Luke 21:37—22:13
W	A.M. 101, 109:1-4, 20-30 P.M. 119:121-144	1 Sam. 7:2-17	Acts 6:1-15	Luke 22:14-23
T	A.M. 105:1-22 P.M. 105:23-45	1 Sam. 8:1-22	Acts 6:15—7:16	Luke 22:24-30
F	A.M. 102 P.M. 107:1-32	1 Sam. 9:1-14	Acts 7:17-29	Luke 22:31-38
S	A.M. 107:33-43, 108:1-6 P.M. 33	1 Sam. 9:15—10:1	Acts 7:30-43	Luke 22:39-51
Week 8 (Week of Sunday Closest to June 29)				
S	A.M. 118 P.M. 145	1 Sam. 10:1-16	Rom. 4:13-25	Matt. 21:23-32

	Psalm	Old Testament	Epistle	Gospel
M	A.M. 106:1-18 P.M. 106:19-48	1 Sam. 10:17-27	Acts 7:44—8:1	Luke 22:52-62
T	A.M. 121, 122, 123 P.M. 124, 125, 126	1 Sam. 11:1-15	Acts 8:1-13	Luke 22:63-71
W	A.M. 119:145-176 P.M. 128, 129, 130	1 Sam. 12:1-6, 16-25	Acts 8:14-25	Luke 23:1-12
T	A.M. 131, 132 P.M. 134, 135	1 Sam. 13:5-18	Acts 8:26-40	Luke 23:13-25
F	A.M. 140, 142 P.M. 141, 143:1-11	1 Sam. 13:19—14:15	Acts 9:1-9	Luke 23:26-31
S	A.M. 137:1-6, 144 P.M. 104	1 Sam. 14:16-30	Acts 9:10-19	Luke 23:32-43

Week 9 (Week of the Sunday Closest to July 6)

	Psalm	Old Testament	Epistle	Gospel
S	A.M. 146, 147 P.M. 111, 112, 113	1 Sam. 14:36-45	Rom. 5:1-11	Matt. 22:1-14
M	A.M. 1, 2, 3 P.M. 4, 7	1 Sam. 15:1-3, 7-23	Acts 9:19-31	Luke 23:44-56
T	A.M. 5, 6 P.M. 10, 11	1 Sam. 15:24-35	Acts 9:32-43	Luke 23:56—24:11
W	A.M. 119:1-24 P.M. 12, 13, 14	1 Sam. 16:1-13	Acts 10:1-16	Luke 24:12-35
T	A.M. 18:1-20 P.M. 18:21-50	1 Sam. 16:14—17:11	Acts 10:17-33	Luke 24:36-53
F	A.M. 16, 17 P.M. 22	1 Sam. 17:17-30	Acts 10:34-48	Mark 1:1-13
S	A.M. 20, 21:1-7 P.M. 110:1-5, 116, 117	1 Sam. 17:31-49	Acts 11:1-18	Mark 1:14-28

Week 10 (Week of the Sunday Closest to July 13)

	Psalm	Old Testament	Epistle	Gospel
S	A.M. 148, 149, 150 P.M. 114, 115	1 Sam. 17:50—18:4	Rom. 10:4-17	Matt. 23:29-39
M	A.M. 25 P.M. 9, 15	1 Sam. 18:5-16, 27-30	Acts 11:19-30	Mark 1:29-45
T	A.M. 26, 28 P.M. 36, 39	1 Sam. 19:1-18	Acts 12:1-17	Mark 2:1-12
W	A.M. 38 P.M. 119:25-48	1 Sam. 20:1-23	Acts 12:18-25	Mark 2:13-22
T	A.M. 37:1-18 P.M. 37:19-42	1 Sam. 20:24-42	Acts 13:1-12	Mark 2:23—3:6
F	A.M. 31 P.M. 35	1 Sam. 21:1-15	Acts 13:13-25	Mark 3:7-19
S	A.M. 30, 32 P.M. 42, 43	1 Sam. 22:1-23	Acts 23:26-43	Mark 3:19-35

Week 11 (Week of the Sunday Closest to July 20)

	Psalm	Old Testament	Epistle	Gospel
S	A.M. 63:1-8, 98 P.M. 103	1 Sam. 23:7-18	Rom. 11:33—12:2	Matt. 25:14-30
M	A.M. 41, 52 P.M. 44	1 Sam. 24:1-22	Acts 13:44-52	Mark 4:1-20
T	A.M. 45 P.M. 47, 48	1 Sam. 25:1-22	Acts 14:1-18	Mark 4:21-34

	Psalm	Old Testament	Epistle	Gospel
W	A.M. 119:49-72 P.M. 49	1 Sam. 25:23-44	Acts 14:19-28	Mark 4:35-41
T	A.M. 50 P.M. 66, 67	1 Sam. 28:3-20	Acts 15:1-11	Mark 5:1-20
F	A.M. 40, 54 P.M. 51	1 Sam. 31:1-13	Acts 15:12-21	Mark 5:21-43
S	A.M. 55 P.M. 138, 139:1-17	2 Sam. 1:1-16	Acts 15:22-35	Mark 6:1-13

Week 12 (Week of the Sunday Closest to July 27)

	Psalm	Old Testament	Epistle	Gospel
S	A.M. 24, 29 P.M. 8, 84	2 Sam. 1:17-27	Rom. 12:9-21	Matt. 25:31-46
M	A.M. 56, 57 P.M. 64, 65	2 Sam. 2:1-11	Acts 15:36—16:5	Mark 6:14-29
T	A.M. 61, 62 P.M. 68:1-20, 24-36	2 Sam. 3:6-21	Acts 16:6-15	Mark 6:30-46
W	A.M. 72 P.M. 119:73-96	2 Sam. 3:22-39	Acts 16:16-24	Mark 6:47-56
T	A.M. 71 P.M. 74	2 Sam. 4:1-12	Acts 16:25-40	Mark 7:1-23
F	A.M. 69:1-23,31-38 P.M. 73	2 Sam. 5:1-12	Acts 17:1-15	Mark 7:24-37
S	A.M. 75, 76 P.M. 23, 27	2 Sam. 5:22—6:11	Acts 17:16-34	Mark 8:1-10

Week 13 (Week of the Sunday Closest to August 3)

	Psalm	Old Testament	Epistle	Gospel
S	A.M. 93, 96 P.M. 34	2 Sam. 6:12-23	Rom. 4:7-12	John 1:43-51
M	A.M. 80 P.M. 77	2 Sam. 7:1-17	Acts 18:1-11	Mark 8:11-21
T	A.M. 78:1-39 P.M. 78:40-72	2 Sam. 7:18-29	Acts 18:12-28	Mark 8:22-33
W	A.M. 119:97-120 P.M. 81, 82	2 Sam. 9:1-13	Acts 19:1-10	Mark 8:34—9:1
T	A.M. 145 P.M. 85, 86	2 Sam. 11:1-27	Acts 19:11-20	Mark 9:2-13
F	A.M. 88 P.M. 91, 92	2 Sam. 12:1-14	Acts 19:21-41	Mark 9:14-29
S	A.M. 87, 90 P.M. 136	2 Sam. 12:15-31	Acts 20:1-16	Mark 9:30-41

Week 14 (Week of the Sunday Closest to August 10)

	Psalm	Old Testament	Epistle	Gospel
S	A.M. 66, 67 P.M. 19, 46	2 Sam. 13:1-22	Rom. 15:1-13	John 3:22-36
M	A.M. 89:1-18 P.M. 89:19-52	2 Sam. 13:23-39	Acts 20:17-38	Mark 9:42-50
T	A.M. 97, 99 P.M. 94	2 Sam. 14:1-20	Acts 21:1-14	Mark 10:1-16
W	A.M. 101, 109:1-4, 20-30 P.M. 119:121-144	2 Sam. 14:21-33	Acts 21:15-26	Mark 10:17-31
T	A.M. 105:1-22 P.M. 105:23-45	2 Sam. 15:1-18	Acts 21:27-36	Mark 10:32-45

	Psalm	Old Testament	Epistle	Gospel
F	A.M. 102 P.M. 107:1-32	2 Sam. 15:19-37	Acts 21:37—22:16	Mark 10:46-52
S	A.M. 107:33-43, 108:1-6 P.M. 33	2 Sam. 16:1-23	Acts 22:17-29	Mark 11:1-11

Week 15 (Week of the Sunday Closest to August 17)

	Psalm	Old Testament	Epistle	Gospel
S	A.M. 118 P.M. 145	2 Sam. 17:1-23	Gal. 3:6-14	John 5:30-47
M	A.M. 106:1-18 P.M. 106:19-48	2 Sam. 17:24—18:8	Acts 22:30—23:11	Mark 11:12-26
T	A.M. 121, 122, 123 P.M. 124, 125, 126	2 Sam. 18:9-18	Acts 23:12-24	Mark 11:27—12:12
W	A.M. 119:145-176 P.M. 128, 129, 130	2 Sam. 18:19-23	Acts 23:23-35	Mark 12:13-27
T	A.M. 131, 132 P.M. 134, 135	2 Sam. 19:1-23	Acts 24:1-23	Mark 12:28-34
F	A.M. 140, 142 P.M. 141, 143:1-11	2 Sam. 19:24-43	Acts 24:24—25:12	Mark 12:35-44
S	A.M. 137:1-6 144 P.M. 104	2 Sam. 23:1-17, 13-17	Acts 25:13-27	Mark 13:1-13

Week 16 (Week of the Sunday Closest to August 24)

	Psalm	Old Testament	Epistle	Gospel
S	A.M. 146, 147 P.M. 111, 112, 113	2 Sam. 24:1-2, 10-25	Gal. 3:23—4:7	John 8:12-20
M	A.M. 1, 2, 3 P.M. 4, 7	1 Kings 1:5-31	Acts 26:1-23	Mark 13:14-27
T	A.M. 5, 6 P.M. 10, 11	1 Kings 1:38—2:4	Acts 26:24—27:8	Mark 13:28-37
W	A.M. 119:1-24 P.M. 12, 13, 14	1 Kings 3:1-15	Acts 27:9-26	Mark 14:1-11
T	A.M. 18:1-20 P.M. 18:21-50	1 Kings 3:16-28	Acts 27:27-44	Mark 14:12-26
F	A.M. 16, 17 P.M. 22	1 Kings 5:1—6:1, 7	Acts 28:1-16	Mark 14:27-42
S	A.M. 20, 21:1-7 P.M. 110:1-5, 116, 117	1 Kings 7:51—8:21	Acts 28:17-31	Mark 14:43-52

Week 17 (Week of the Sunday Closest to August 31)

	Psalm	Old Testament	Epistle	Gospel
S	A.M. 148, 149, 150 P.M. 114, 115	1 Kings 8:22-30	1 Tim. 4:7-16	John 8:47-59
M	A.M. 25 P.M. 9, 15	2 Chron. 6:32—7:7	James 2:1-13	Mark 14:53-65
T	A.M. 26, 28 P.M. 36, 39	1 Kings 8:65—9:9	James 2:14-26	Mark 14:66-72
W	A.M. 38 P.M. 119:25-48	1 Kings 9:24—10:13	James 3:1-12	Mark 15:1-11
T	A.M. 37:1-18 P.M. 37:19-42	1 Kings 11:1-13	James 3:13—4:12	Mark 15:12-21
F	A.M. 31 P.M. 35	1 Kings 11:26-43	James 4:13—5:6	Mark 15:22-32
S	A.M. 30, 32 P.M. 42, 43	1 Kings 12:1-20	James 5:7-12, 19-20	Mark 15:33-39

	Psalm	Old Testament	Epistle	Gospel
Week 18 (Week of the Sunday Closest to September 7)				
S	A.M. 63:1-8, 98 P.M. 103	1 Kings 12:21-33	Acts 4:18-31	John 10:31-42
M	A.M. 41, 52 P.M. 44	1 Kings 13:1-10	Phil. 1:1-11	Mark 15:40-47
T	A.M. 45 P.M. 47, 48	1 Kings 16:23-34	Phil. 1:12-30	Mark 16:1-8
M	A.M. 119:49-72 P.M. 49	1 Kings 17:1-24	Phil. 2:1-11	Matt. 2:1-12
T	A.M. 50 P.M. 93, 96	1 Kings 18:1-19	Phil. 2:12-30	Matt. 2:13-23
F	A.M. 40, 54 P.M. 51	1 Kings 18:20-40	Phil. 3:1-16	Matt. 3:1-12
S	A.M. 55 P.M. 138, 139:1-17	1 Kings 18:41—19:8	Phil. 3:17—4:7	Matt. 3:13-17
Week 19 (Week of the Sunday Closest to September 14)				
S	A.M. 24, 29 P.M. 8, 84	1 Kings 19:8-21	Acts 5:34-42	John 11:45-47
M	A.M. 56, 57 P.M. 64, 65	1 Kings 21:1-16	1 Cor. 1:1-19	Matt. 4:1-11
T	A.M. 61, 62 P.M. 68:1-20, 24-36	1 Kings 21:17-29	1 Cor. 1:20-31	Matt. 4:12-17
W	A.M. 72 P.M. 119:73-96	1 Kings 22:1-28	1 Cor. 2:1-13	Matt. 4:18-25
T	A.M. 71 P.M. 74	1 Kings 22:29-45	1 Cor. 2:14—3:15	Matt. 5:1-10
F	A.M. 69:1-23, 31-38 P.M. 73	2 Kings 1:2-17	1 Cor. 3:16-23	Matt. 5:11-16
S	A.M. 75, 76 P.M. 23, 27	2 Kings 2:1-18	1 Cor. 4:1-7	Matt. 5:17-20
Week 20 (Week of the Sunday Closest to September 21)				
S	A.M. 93, 96 P.M. 34	2 Kings 4:8-37	Acts 9:10-31	Luke 3:7-18
M	A.M. 80 P.M. 77	2 Kings 5:1-19	1 Cor. 4:8-21	Matt. 5:21-26
T	A.M. 78:1-39 P.M. 78:40-72	2 Kings 5:19-27	1 Cor. 5:1-8	Matt. 5:27-37
W	A.M. 119:97-120 P.M. 81, 82	2 Kings 6:1-23	1 Cor. 5:9—6:8	Matt. 5:38-48
T	A.M. 146, 147 P.M. 85, 86	2 Kings 9:1-16	1 Cor. 6:12-20	Matt. 6:1-6, 16-18
F	A.M. 88 P.M. 91, 92	2 Kings 9:17-37	1 Cor. 7:1-9	Matt. 6:7-15
S	A.M. 87, 90 P.M. 136	2 Kings 11:1-20	1 Cor. 7:10-24	Matt. 6:19-24
Week 21 (Week of the Sunday Closest to September 28)				
S	A.M. 66, 67 P.M. 19, 46	2 Kings 17:1-18	Acts 9:36-43	Luke 5:1-11

	Psalm	Old Testament	Epistle	Gospel
M	A.M. 89:1-18 P.M. 89:19-52	2 Kings 17:24-41	1 Cor. 7:25-31	Matt. 6:25-34
T	A.M. 97, 99 P.M. 94	2 Chron. 29:1-3, 30:1, 10-27	1 Cor. 7:32-40	Matt. 7:1-12
W	A.M. 101, 109:1-4, 20-30 P.M. 119:121-144	2 Kings 18:9-25	1 Cor. 8:1-13	Matt. 7:13-21
T	A.M. 105:1-22 P.M. 105:23-45	2 Kings 18:28-37	1 Cor. 9:1-15	Matt. 7:22-29
F	A.M. 102 P.M. 107:1-32	2 Kings 19:1-20	1 Cor. 9:16-27	Matt. 8:1-17
S	A.M. 107:33-43, 108:1-6 P.M. 33	2 Kings 19:21-36	1 Cor. 10:1-13	Matt. 8:18-27

Week 22 (Week of the Sunday Closest to October 5)

	Psalm	Old Testament	Epistle	Gospel
S	A.M. 118 P.M. 145	2 Kings 20:1-21	Acts 12:1-17	Luke 7:11-17
M	A.M. 106:1-18 P.M. 106:19-48	2 Kings 21:1-18	1 Cor. 10:14—11:1	Matt. 8:28-34
T	A.M. 121, 122, 123 P.M. 124, 125, 126	2 Kings 22:1-13	1 Cor. 11:2, 17-22	Matt. 9:1-8
M	A.M. 119:145-176 P.M. 128, 129, 130	2 Kings 22:14—23:3	1 Cor. 11:23-34	Matt. 9:9-17
T	A.M. 131, 132 P.M. 134, 135	2 Kings 23:4-25	1 Cor. 12:1-11	Matt. 9:18-26
F	A.M. 140, 142 P.M. 141, 143:1-11	2 Kings 23:36—24:17	1 Cor. 12:12-26	Matt. 9:27-34
S	A.M. 137:1-6, 144 P.M. 104	Jer. 35:1-19	1 Cor. 12:27—13:3	Matt. 9:35—10:4

Week 23 (Week of the Sunday Closest to October 12)

	Psalm	Old Testament	Epistle	Gospel
S	A.M. 146, 147 P.M. 111, 112, 113	Jer. 36:1-10	Acts 14:8-18	Luke 7:36-50
M	A.M. 1, 2, 3 P.M. 4, 7	Jer. 36:11-26	1 Cor. 13:4-13	Matt. 10:5-15
T	A.M. 5, 6 P.M. 10, 11	Jer. 36:27—37:2	1 Cor. 14:1-12	Matt. 10:16-23
W	A.M. 119:1-24 P.M. 12, 13, 14	Jer. 37:3-21	1 Cor. 14:13-25	Matt. 10:24-33
T	A.M. 18:1-20 P.M. 18:21-50	Jer. 38:1-13	1 Cor. 14:26-33, 37-40	Matt. 10:34-42
F	A.M. 16, 17 P.M. 22	Jer. 38:14-28	1 Cor. 15:1-11	Matt. 11:1-6
S	A.M. 20, 21:1-7 P.M. 110:1-5, 116, 117	2 Kings 25:8-12, 22-26	1 Cor. 15:12-29	Matt. 11:7-15

Week 24 (Week of the Sunday Closest to October 19)

	Psalm	Old Testament	Epistle	Gospel
S	A.M. 148, 149, 150 P.M. 114, 115	Jer. 29:1, 4-14	Acts 16:6-15	Luke 10:1-12, 17-20
M	A.M. 25 P.M. 9, 15	Jer. 44:1-14	1 Cor. 15:30-41	Matt. 11:16-24
T	A.M. 26, 28 P.M. 36, 39	Lam. 1:1-5, 10-12	1 Cor. 15:41-50	Matt. 11:25-30

	Psalm	Old Testament	Epistle	Gospel
W	A.M. 38 P.M. 119:25-48	Lam. 2:8-15	1 Cor. 15:51-58	Matt. 12:1-14
T	A.M. 37:1-18 P.M. 37:19-42	Ezra 1:1-11	1 Cor. 16:1-9	Matt. 12:15-21
F	A.M. 31 P.M. 35	Ezra 3:1-13	1 Cor 16:10-24	Matt. 12:22-32
S	A.M. 30, 32 P.M. 42, 43	Ezra 4:7, 11-24	Philem. 1-25	Matt. 12:33-42

Week 25 (Week of the Sunday Closest to October 26)

	Psalm	Old Testament	Epistle	Gospel
S	A.M. 63:1-8, 98 P.M. 103	Hag. 1:1—2:9	Acts 18:24—19:7	Luke 10:25-37
M	A.M. 41, 52 P.M. 44	Zech. 1:7-17	Rev. 1:4-20	Matt. 12:43-50
T	A.M. 45 P.M. 47, 48	Ezra 5:1-17	Rev. 4:1-11	Matt. 13:1-9
W	A.M. 119:49-72 P.M. 49	Ezra 6:1-22	Rev. 5:1-10	Matt. 13:10-17
T	A.M. 50 P.M. 33	Neh. 1:1-11	Rev. 5:11—6:11	Matt. 13:18-23
F	A.M. 40, 54 P.M. 51	Neh. 2:1-20	Rev. 6:12—7:4	Matt. 13:24-30
S	A.M. 55 P.M. 138, 139:1-17	Neh. 4:1-23	Rev. 7:9-17	Matt. 13:31-35

Week 26 (Week of the Sunday Closest to November 2)

	Psalm	Old Testament	Epistle	Gospel
S	A.M. 24, 29 P.M. 8, 84	Neh. 5:1-19	Acts 20:7-12	Luke 12:22-31
M	A.M. 56, 57 P.M. 64, 65	Neh. 6:1-19	Rev. 10:1-11	Matt. 13:36-43
T	A.M. 61, 62 P.M. 68:1-20, 24-36	Neh. 12:27-31, 42-47	Rev. 11:1-19	Matt. 13:44-52
W	A.M. 72 P.M. 119:73-96	Neh. 13:4-22	Rev. 12:1-12	Matt. 13:53-58
T	A.M. 71 P.M. 74	Ezra 7:11-26	Rev. 14:1-13	Matt. 14:1-12
F	A.M. 69:1-23, 31-38 P.M. 73	Ezra 7:27-28, 8:21-36	Rev. 15:1-8	Matt. 14:13-21
S	A.M. 75, 76 P.M. 23, 27	Ezra 9:1-15	Rev. 17:1-14	Matt. 14:22-36

Week 27 (Week of the Sunday Closest to November 9)

	Psalm	Old Testament	Epistle	Gospel
S	A.M. 93, 96 P.M. 34	Ezra 10:1-17	Acts 24:10-21	Luke 14:12-24
M	A.M. 80 P.M. 77	Neh. 9:1-15	Rev. 18:1-8	Matt. 15:1-20
T	A.M. 78:1-39 P.M. 78:40-72	Neh. 9:26-38	Rev. 18:9-20	Matt. 15:21-28
W	A.M. 119:97-120 P.M. 81, 82	Neh. 7:7—8:3, 5-18	Rev. 18:21-24	Matt. 15:29-39
T	A.M. 23, 27 P.M. 85, 86	Amos 5:18-24	Rev. 19:1-10	Matt. 16:1-12

	Psalm	Old Testament	Epistle	Gospel
F	A.M. 88 P.M. 91, 92	Zeph. 1:7, 12-18	Rev. 19:11-16	Matt. 16:13-20
S	A.M. 87, 90 P.M. 136	Ezek. 34:11-17	Rev. 20:1-6	Mark 16:21-28

Week 28 (Week of the Sunday Closest to November 16)

	Psalm	Old Testament	Epistle	Gospel
S	A.M. 66, 67 P.M. 19, 46	Ezek. 34:11-17	Acts 28:14-23	Luke 16:1-13
M	A.M. 89:1-18 P.M. 89:19-52	1 Kings 17:8-16	Rev. 20:7-15	Matt. 17:1-13
T	A.M. 97, 99 P.M. 94	2 Sam. 7:4, 8-16	Rev. 21:1-8	Matt. 17:14-21
W	A.M. 101, 109:1-4, 20-30 P.M. 119:121-144	Mal. 3:13—4:2, 5-6	Rev. 21:9-21	Matt. 17:22-27
T	A.M. 105:1-22 P.M. 105:23-45	Isa. 64:1-9	Rev. 21:22—22:5	Matt. 18:1-9
F	A.M. 102 P.M. 107:1-32	Isa. 40:1-11	Rev. 22:6-13	Matt. 18:10-20
S	A.M. 107:33-43, 108:1-6 P.M. 33	Isa. 65:17-25	Rev. 22:14-21	Matt. 18:21-35

Week 29 (Week of the Sunday Closest to November 23)

	Psalm	Old Testament	Epistle	Gospel
S	A.M. 118 P.M. 145	Isa. 19:19-25	Rom. 15:5-13	Luke 19:11-27
M	A.M. 106:1-18 P.M. 106:19-48	Joel 3:1-2, 9-17	1 Pet. 1:1-12	Matt. 19:1-12
T	A.M. 121, 122, 123 P.M. 124, 125, 126	Nahum 1:1-13	1 Pet. 1:13-25	Matt. 19:13-22
W	A.M. 119:145-176 P.M. 128, 129, 130	Obadiah 15-21	1 Pet. 2:1-10	Matt. 19:23-30
T	A.M. 131, 132 P.M. 134, 135	Zeph. 3:1-13	1 Pet. 2:11-25	Matt. 20:1-16
F	A.M. 140, 142 P.M. 141, 143:1-11	Isa. 24:14-23	1 Pet. 3:13—4:6	Matt. 20:17-28
S	A.M. 137:1-6, 144 P.M. 104	Mic. 7:11-20	1 Pet. 4:7-19	Matt. 20:29-34

YEAR TWO

	Psalm	Old Testament	Epistle	Gospel
Week 1 Advent				
S	A.M. 146, 147 P.M. 111, 112, 113	Amos 1:1-5, 13—2:8	1 Thess. 5:1-11	Luke 21:5-19
M	A.M. 1, 2, 3 P.M. 4, 7	Amos 2:6-16	2 Pet. 1:1-11	Matt. 21:1-11
T	A.M. 5, 6 P.M. 10, 11	Amos 3:1-11	2 Pet. 1:12-21	Matt. 21:12-22
W	A.M. 119:1-24 P.M. 12, 13, 14	Amos 3:12—4:5	2 Pet. 3:1-10	Matt. 21:23-32
T	A.M. 18:1-20 P.M. 18:21-50	Amos 4:6-13	2 Pet. 3:11-18	Matt. 21:33-46
F	A.M. 16, 17 P.M. 22	Amos 5:1-17	Jude 1-16	Matt. 22:1-14
S	A.M. 20, 21:1-7 P.M. 110:1-5, 116, 117	Amos 5:18-27	Jude 17-25	Matt. 22:15-22
Week 2 Advent				
S	A.M. 148, 149, 150 P.M. 114, 115	Amos 6:1-14	1 Thess. 5:1-11	Luke 1:57-68
M	A.M. 25 P.M. 9, 15	Amos 7:1-9	Rev. 1:1-8	Matt. 22:23-33
T	A.M. 26, 28 P.M. 36, 39	Amos 7:10-17, 24-25	Rev. 1:9-16	Matt. 22:34-46
W	A.M. 38 P.M. 119:25-48	Amos 8:1-14	Rev. 1:17—2:7	Matt. 23:1-12
T	A.M. 37:1-18 P.M. 37:19-42	Amos 9:1-10	Rev. 2:8-17	Matt. 23:13-26
F	A.M. 31 P.M. 35	Hag. 1:1-15	Rev. 2:18-29	Matt. 23:27-39
S	A.M. 30, 32 P.M. 42, 43	Hag. 2:1-19	Rev. 3:1-6	Matt. 24:1-14
Week 3 Advent				
S	A.M. 63:1-8, 98 P.M. 103	Amos 9:11-15	2 Thess. 2:1-3, 13-17	John 5:30-47
M	A.M. 41, 52 P.M. 44	Zech. 1:7-17	Rev. 3:7-13	Matt. 24:15-31
T	A.M. 45 P.M. 47, 48	Zech. 2:1-13	Rev. 3:14-22	Matt. 24:32-44
W	A.M. 119:49-72 P.M. 49	Zech. 3:1-10	Rev. 4:1-8	Matt. 24:45-51
T	A.M. 50 P.M. 33	Zech. 4:1-14	Rev. 4:9—5:5	Matt. 25:1-13
F	A.M. 40, 54 P.M. 51	Zech. 7:8—8:8	Rev. 5:6-14	Matt. 25:14-30
S	A.M. 55 P.M. 138, 139:1-17	Zech. 8:9-17	Rev. 6:1-17	Matt. 25:31-46

	Psalm	Old Testament	Epistle	Gospel
Week 4 Advent				
S	A.M. 24, 29 P.M. 8, 84	Gen. 3:18-15	Rev. 12:1-10	John 3:16-21
M	A.M. 61, 62 P.M. 112, 115	Zeph. 3:14-20	Titus 1:1-16	Luke 1:1-25
T	A.M. 66, 67 P.M. 116, 117	1 Sam. 2:1-10	Titus 2:1-10	Luke 1:26-38
W	A.M. 72 P.M. 111, 113	2 Sam. 7:1-17	Titus 2:11—3:8	Luke 1:39-48
T	A.M. 80 P.M. 146, 147	2 Sam. 7:18-29	Gal. 3:1-14	Luke 1:57-66
F	A.M. 93, 96 P.M. 148, 150	Isa. 7:10-17	Gal. 3:15-22	Luke 1:67-80 or Matt. 1:1-17
Dec. 24				
	A.M. 45, 46	Isa. 9:2-7	Gal. 3:23-4:7	Matt. 1:18-25
Christmas Eve				
	A.M. 89:1-29	Isa. 59:15-21	Phil. 2:5-11	
Christmas Day and Following				
Christmas Day				
	A.M. 2, 85 P.M. 110:1-1, 132	Mic. 4:1-5, 5:2-4	1 John 4:7-16	Matt. 2:1-12, John 3:31-26
First Sunday after Christmas				
	A.M. 93, 96 P.M. 34	1 Sam. 1:1-2, 7-28	Heb 2:10-18	Matt. 1:18-25
Dec. 29				
	A.M. 18:1-20 P.M. 18:21-50*	2 Sam. 23:13-17	Rev. 1:1-8	John 7:37-52
*If today is Saturday, use Ps. 23 and 27 at evening prayer				
Dec. 30				
	A.M. 20, 21:1-7 P.M. 23, 27	1 Kings 17:17-24	Rev. 1:9-20	John 7:53—8:11
Dec. 31				
	A.M. 46, 48	1 Kings 3:5-14	2 Cor. 5:16—6:2	John 8:12-19
Eve of Holy Name				
	A.M. 90	Isa. 65:15-25	Rev. 21:1-6	
Holy Name				
	A.M. 103 P.M. 148	Isa. 62:1-5, 10-12	Col. 2:6-12	John 16:23-30
Second Sunday after Christmas				
	A.M. 66, 67 P.M. 145	Isa. 61:10	Col. 3:12-17	John 6:41-47
Jan. 2				
	A.M. 34 P.M. 33	1 Kings 19:1-8	Eph. 4:1-16	John 6:1-14

	Psalm	Old Testament	Epistle	Gospel
Jan. 3				
	A.M. 68 P.M. 72**	1 Kings 19:9-18	Eph. 4:17-32	John 6:15-27
If today is Saturday, use Ps. 136 at evening prayer.				
Jan. 4				
	A.M. 85,87 P.M. 89:1-29**	Josh. 3:14—4:7	Eph. 5:1-20	John 9:1-12, 35-38
If today is Saturday, use Ps. 136 at evening prayer.				
Jan. 5				
	A.M. 2, 110:1-5	Jon. 2:2-9	Eph. 6:10-20	John 11:17-27, 38-44
Eve of Epiphany				
	A.M. 29, 98	Isa. 66:18-23	Rom. 15:7-13	

The Epiphany
(Begins on January 6 and lasts until Lent)

	Psalm	Old Testament	Epistle	Gospel
Epiphany				
	A.M. 46, 97 P.M. 96, 100	Isa. 49:1-7	Rev. 21:22-27	Matt. 12:14-21
Jan. 7				
	A.M. 103 P.M. 114, 115	Deut. 8:1-3	Col. 1:1-14	John 6:30-33, 48-51
Jan. 8				
	A.M. 117, 118 P.M. 112, 113	Exod. 17:1-7	Col. 1:15-23	John 7:37-52
Jan. 9				
	A.M. 121, 122, 123 P.M. 131, 132	Isa. 45:14-19	Col. 1:24-2:7	John 8:12-19
Jan. 10				
	A.M. 138, 139:1-17 P.M. 147	Jer. 23:1-8	Col. 2:8-23	John 10:7-17
Jan. 11				
	A.M. 148, 150 P.M. 91, 92	Isa. 55:3-9	Col. 3:1-17	John 14:6-14
Jan. 12				
	A.M. 98, 99	Gen. 49:1-2, 8-12	Col 3:18—4:6	John 15:1-16
Eve of 1 Epiphany				
	A.M. 104	Isa. 61:1-9	Gal. 3:23-29, 4:4-7	
Week 1 Epiphany				
S	A.M. 146, 147 P.M. 111, 112, 113	Gen. 1:1—2:3	Eph. 1:3-14	John 1:29-34
M	A.M. 1, 2, 3 P.M. 4, 7	Gen. 2:4-9, 16-25	Heb. 1:1-14	John 1:1-18
T	A.M. 5, 6 P.M. 10, 11	Gen. 3:1-24	Heb. 2:1-10	John 1:19-28
W	A.M. 119:1-24 P.M. 12, 13, 14	Gen. 4:1-16	Heb. 2:11-18	John 1:35-42

	Psalm	Old Testament	Epistle	Gospel
T	A.M. 18:1-20 P.M. 18:21-50	Gen. 4:17-26	Heb. 3:1-11	John 1:43-51
F	A.M. 16, 17 P.M. 22	Gen. 6:1-8	Heb. 3:12-19	John 2:1-12
S	A.M. 20, 21:1-7 P.M. 110:1-5, 116, 117	Gen. 6:9-22	Heb. 4:1-13	John 2:13-22
Week 2 Epiphany				
S	A.M. 148, 149, 150 P.M. 114, 115	Gen. 7:1-10, 17-23	Eph. 4:1-16	Mark 3:7-19
M	A.M. 25 P.M. 9, 15	Gen. 8:6-22	Heb. 4:14—5:6	John 2:23—3:15
T	A.M. 26, 28 P.M. 36, 39	Gen. 9:1-17	Heb. 5:7-14	John 3:16-21
W	A.M. 38 P.M. 119:25-48	Gen. 9:18-29	Heb. 6:1-12	John 3:22-36
T	A.M. 37:1-18 P.M. 37:19-42	Gen. 11:1-9	Heb. 6:13-20	John 4:1-15
F	A.M. 31 P.M. 35	Gen. 11:27—12:8	Heb. 7:1-17	John 4:16-26
S	A.M. 30, 32 P.M. 42, 43	Gen. 12:9—13:1	Heb. 7:18-28	John 4:27-42
Week 3 Epiphany				
S	A.M. 63:1-8, P.M. 98, 103	Gen. 13:2-18	Gal. 2:1-10	Mark 7:31-37
M	A.M. 41, 52 P.M. 44	Gen. 14:8-24	Heb. 8:1-13	John 4:43-54
T	A.M. 45 P.M. 47,48	Gen. 15:1-11, 17-21	Heb. 9:1-14	John 5:1-18
W	A.M. 119:49-72 P.M. 49	Gen. 16:1-14	Heb. 9:15-28	John 5:19-29
T	A.M. 50 P.M. 118	Gen. 16:15—17:14	Heb. 10:1-10	John 5:30-47
F	A.M. 40, 54 P.M. 51	Gen. 17:15-27	Heb. 10:11-25	John 6:1-15
S	A.M. 55 P.M. 138, 139:1-17	Gen. 18:1-16	Heb. 10:26-39	John 6:16-27
Week 4 Epiphany				
S	A.M. 24, 29 P.M. 8, 84	Gen. 18:16-33	Gal. 5:13-25	Mark 8:22-30
M	A.M. 56, 57 P.M. 64, 65	Gen. 19:1-17, 24-29	Heb. 11:1-12	John 6:27-40
T	A.M. 61, 62 P.M. 68:1-20, 24-36	Gen. 21:1-21	Heb. 11:13-22	John 6:41-51
W	A.M. 72 P.M. 119:73-96	Gen. 22:1-18	Heb. 11:23-31	John 6:52-59
T	A.M. 71 P.M. 74	Gen. 23:1-20	Heb. 11:32—12:2	John 6:60-71
F	A.M. 69:1-23, 31-38 P.M. 73	Gen. 24:1-27	Heb. 12:3-11	John 7:1-13

	Psalm	Old Testament	Epistle	Gospel
S	A.M. 75, 76 P.M. 23, 27	Gen. 24:28-38, 49-51	Heb. 12:12-29	John 7:14-36

Week 5 Epiphany

	Psalm	Old Testament	Epistle	Gospel
S	A.M. 93, 96 P.M. 34	Gen. 24:50-67	2 Tim. 2:14-21	Mark 10:13-22
M	A.M. 80 P.M. 77	Gen. 25:19-34	Heb. 13:1-16	John 7:37-52
T	A.M. 78:1-39 P.M. 78:40-72	Gen. 26:1-6, 12-33	Heb. 13:17-25	John 7:53—8:11
W	A.M. 119:97-120 P.M. 81, 82	Gen. 27:1-29	Rom. 12:1-8	John 8:12-20
T	A.M. 146, 147 P.M. 85, 86	Gen. 27:30-45	Rom. 12:9-21	John 8:21-32
F	A.M. 88 P.M. 91, 92	Gen. 27:46—28:4, 10-22	Rom. 13:1-14	John 8:33-47
S	A.M. 87, 90 P.M. 136	Gen. 29:1-20	Rom. 14:1-23	John 8:47-59

Week 6 Epiphany

	Psalm	Old Testament	Epistle	Gospel
S	A.M. 66, 67 P.M. 19, 46	Gen. 29:20-35	1 Tim. 3:14—4:10	Mark 10:23-31
M	A.M. 89:1-18 P.M. 89:19-52	Gen. 30:1-24	1 John 1:1-10	John 9:1-17
T	A.M. 97, 99 P.M. 94	Gen. 31:1-24	1 John 2:1-11	John 9:18-41
W	A.M. 101, 109:1-4, 20-30 P.M. 119:121-144	Gen. 31:25-50	1 John 2:12-17	John 10:1-18
T	A.M. 105:1-22 P.M. 105:23-45	Gen. 32:3-21	1 John 2:18-29	John 10:19-30
F	A.M. 102 P.M. 107:1-32	Gen. 32:22—33:17	1 John 3:1-10	John 10:31-42
S	A.M. 107:33-43, 108:1-6 P.M. 33	Gen. 35:1-20	1 John 3:11-18	John 11:1-16

Week 7 Epiphany

	Psalm	Old Testament	Epistle	Gospel
S	A.M. 118 P.M. 145	Prov. 1:20-33	2 Cor. 5:11-21	Mark 10:35-45
M	A.M. 106:1-18 P.M. 106:19-48	Prov. 3:11-20	1 John 3:18—4:6	John 11:17-29
T	A.M. 121, 122, 123 P.M. 124, 125, 126	Prov. 4:1-27	1 John 4:7-21	John 11:30-44
W	A.M. 119:145-176 P.M. 128, 129, 130	Prov. 6:1-19	1 John 5:1-12	John 11:45-54
T	A.M. 131, 132, P.M. 134, 135	Prov. 7:1-27	1 John 5:13-21	John 11:55—12:8
F	A.M. 140, 142 P.M. 141, 143:1-11	Prov. 8:1-21	Philem. 1-25	John 12:9-19
S	A.M. 137:1-6, 144 P.M. 104	Prov. 8:22-36	2 Tim. 1:1-14	John 12:20-26

	Psalm	Old Testament	Epistle	Gospel
Week 8 Epiphany				
S	A.M. 146, 147 P.M. 111, 112, 113	Prov. 9:1-12	2 Cor. 9:6-15	Mark 10:46-52
M	A.M. 1, 2, 3 P.M. 4, 7	Prov. 10:1-12	2 Tim. 1:15—2:13	John 12:27-36
T	A.M. 5, 6 P.M. 10, 11	Prov. 15:16-33	2 Tim. 2:14-26	John 12:36-50
W	A.M. 119:1-24 P.M. 12, 13, 14	Prov. 17:1-20	2 Tim. 3:1-17	John 13:1-20
T	A.M. 18:1-20 P.M. 18:21-50	Prov. 21:30—22:6	2 Tim. 4:1-8	John 13:21-30
F	A.M. 16, 17 P.M. 22	Prov. 23:19-21, 29—24:2	2 Tim. 4:9-22	John 13:31-38
S	A.M. 20, 21:1-7 P.M. 110:1-5, 116, 117	Prov. 25:15-28	Phil. 1:1-11	John 18:1-14
Week of Last Epiphany				
S	A.M. 148, 149, 150 P.M. 114, 115	Exod. 24:12-18	2 Cor. 3:7-18	Luke 9:18-27
M	A.M. 25 P.M. 9, 15	Prov. 27:1-6, 10-12	Phil. 2:1-13	John 18:15-18, 25-27
T	A.M. 26, 28 P.M. 36, 39	Prov. 30:1-4, 24-33	Phil. 3:1-11	John 18:28-38
Ash Wednesday				
	A.M. 32, 143 P.M. 102, 130	Amos 5:6-15	Heb. 12:1-14	Luke 18:9-14
T	A.M. 37:1-18 P.M. 37:19-42	Hab. 3:1-10, 16-18	Phil. 3:12-21	John 17:1-8
F	A.M. 31 P.M. 35	Ezek. 18:1-4, 25-32	Phil. 4:1-9	John 17:9-19
S	A.M. 30, 32 P.M. 42, 43	Ezek. 39:21-29	Phil. 4:10-20	John 17:20-26

*For the Invitatory

Lent

	Psalm	Old Testament	Epistle	Gospel
Week 1 Lent				
S	A.M. 63:1-8, 98 P.M. 103	Dan. 9:3-10	Heb. 2:10-18	John 12:44-50
M	A.M. 41, 52 P.M. 44	Gen. 37:1-11	1 Cor. 1:1-19	Mark 1:1-13
T	A.M. 45 P.M. 47, 48	Gen. 37:12-24	1 Cor. 1:20-31	Mark 1:14-28
W	A.M. 119:49-72 P.M. 49	Gen. 37:25-36	1 Cor. 2:1-13	Mark 1:29-45
T	A.M. 50 P.M. 19, 46	Gen. 39:1-23	1 Cor. 2:14—3:15	Mark 2:1-12
F	A.M. 40, 54 P.M. 51	Gen. 40:1-23	1 Cor. 3:16-23	Mark 2:13-22
S	A.M. 55 P.M. 138, 139:1-17	Gen. 41:1-13	1 Cor. 4:1-7	Mark 2:23—3:6

	Psalm	Old Testament	Epistle	Gospel
Week 2 Lent				
S	A.M. 24, 29 P.M. 8, 84	Gen. 41:14-45	Rom. 6:3-14	John 5:19-24
M	A.M. 56, 57 P.M. 64, 65	Gen. 41:46-57	1 Cor. 4:8-20	Mark 3:7-19
T	A.M. 61, 62 P.M. 68:1-20, 24-36	Gen. 42:1-17	1 Cor. 5:1-8	Mark 3:19-35
W	A.M. 72 P.M. 119:73-96	Gen. 42:18-28	1 Cor. 5:9—6:8	Mark 4:1-20
T	A.M. 71 P.M. 74	Gen. 42:29-38	1 Cor. 6:12-30	Mark 4:21-34
F	A.M. 69:1-23, 31-38 P.M. 73	Gen. 43:1-15	1 Cor. 7:1-9	Mark 4:35-41
S	A.M. 75, 76 P.M. 23, 27	Gen. 43:16-34	1 Cor. 7:10-24	Mark 5:1-20
Week 3 Lent				
S	A.M. 93, 96 P.M. 34	Gen. 44:1-17	Rom. 8:1-10	John 5:25-29
M	A.M. 80 P.M. 77	Gen. 44:18-34	1 Cor. 7:25-31	Mark 5:21-43
T	A.M. 78:1-39 P.M. 78:40-72	Gen. 45:1-15	1 Cor. 7:32-40	Mark 6:1-13
W	A.M. 119:97-120 P.M. 81, 82	Gen. 45:16-28	1 Cor. 8:1-13	Mark 6:13-29
T	A.M. 42, 43 P.M. 85, 86	Gen. 46:1-7, 28-34	1 Cor. 9:1-15	Mark 6:30-46
F	A.M. 88 P.M. 91, 92	Gen. 47:1-26	1 Cor. 9:16-27	Mark 6:47-56
S	A.M. 87, 90 P.M. 136	Gen. 47:27—48:7	1 Cor. 10:1-13	Mark 7:1-23
Week of 4 Lent				
S	A.M. 66, 67 P.M. 19, 46	Gen. 48:8-22	Rom. 8:11-25	John 6:27-40
M	A.M. 89:1-18 P.M. 89:19-52	Gen. 49:1-28	1 Cor. 10:14—11:1	Mark 7:24-37
T	A.M. 97, 99 P.M. 94	Gen. 49:29—50:14	1 Cor. 11:17-34	Mark 8:1-10
W	A.M. 101, 109:1-4, 20-30 P.M. 119:121-144	Gen. 50:15-26	1 Cor. 12:1-11	Mark 8:11-26
T	A.M. 69:1-23, 31-38 P.M. 73	Exod. 1:6-22	1 Cor. 12:12-26	Mark 8:27—9:1
F	A.M. 102 P.M. 107:1-32	Exod. 2:1-22	1 Cor. 12:27—13:3	Mark 9:2-13
S	A.M. 107:33-43, 108:1-6 P.M. 33	Exod. 2:23—3:15	1 Cor. 13:1-13	Mark 9:14-29
Week 5 Lent				
S	A.M. 118 P.M. 145	Exod. 3:16—4:12	Rom. 12:1-21	John 8:46-59

	Psalm	Old Testament	Epistle	Gospel
M	A.M. 31 P.M. 35	Exod. 4:10-20, 27-31	1 Cor. 14:1-19	Mark 9:30-41
T	A.M. 121, 122, 123 P.M. 124, 125, 126	Exod. 5:1—6:1	1 Cor. 14:20-33, 39-40	Mark 9:42-50
W	A.M. 119:145-176 P.M. 128, 129, 130	Exod. 7:8-24	2 Cor. 2:14—3:6	Mark 10:1-16
T	A.M. 131, 132 P.M. 140, 142	Exod. 7:25—8:19	2 Cor. 3:7-18	Mark 10:17-31
F	A.M. 141 P.M. 143:1-11	Exod. 9:13-35	2 Cor. 4:1-12	Mark 10:32-45
S	A.M. 137:1-6, 144 P.M. 42, 43	Exod. 10:21—11:8	2 Cor. 4:13-18	Mark 10:46-52

Holy Week

Palm Sunday

	Psalm	Old Testament	Epistle	Gospel
	A.M. 24, 29 P.M. 103	Zech. 12:9-11, 13:1, 7-9	1 Tim. 6:12-16	Luke 19:41-48
M	A.M. 51:1-18 P.M. 69:1-23	Lam. 1:1-2, 6-12	2 Cor. 1:1-7	Mark 11:12-25
T	A.M. 6, 12 P.M. 94	Lam. 1:17-22	2 Cor. 1:8-22	Mark 11:27-33
W	A.M. 55 P.M. 74	Lam. 2:1-9, 14-17	2 Cor. 1:23—2:11	Mark 12:1-11

Maundy Thursday

	Psalm	Old Testament	Epistle	Gospel
	A.M. 102 P.M. 142, 143	Lam. 2:10-18	1 Cor. 10:14-17, 11:27-32	Mark 14:12-25

Good Friday

	Psalm	Old Testament	Epistle	Gospel
	A.M. 22 P.M. 40:1-14, 54	Lam. 3:1-9, 19-33	1 Pet. 1:10-20	John 19:38-42

Holy Saturday

	Psalm	Old Testament	Epistle	Gospel
	A.M. 88 P.M. 27	Lam. 3:37-58	Heb. 4:1-16	Rom. 8:1-11

Easter Week

Easter Day

	Psalm	Old Testament	Epistle	Gospel
	A.M. 148, 149, 150 P.M. 113, 114	Isa. 51:9-11	Matt. 28:1-10	Col. 3:1-4
M	A.M. 93, 98 P.M. 66	Exod. 12:14-27	1 Cor. 15:1-11	Mark 16:1-8
T	A.M. 103 P.M. 111, 114	Exod. 12:28-39	1 Cor. 15:12-28	Mark 16:9-20
W	A.M. 97, 99 P.M. 115	Exod. 12:40-51	1 Cor. 15:30-41	Matt. 28:1-16
T	A.M. 146, 147 P.M. 148, 149	Exod. 13:3-10	1 Cor. 15:41-50	Matt. 28:16-20
F	A.M. 136 P.M. 118	Exod. 13:1-2, 11-16	1 Cor. 15:51-58	Luke 24:1-12
S	A.M. 145 P.M. 104	Exod. 13:17-14:4	2 Cor. 4:16—5:10	Mark 12:18-27

	Psalm	Old Testament	Epistle	Gospel
Week 2 Easter				
S	A.M. 146, 147 P.M. 111, 112, 113	Exod. 14:5-22	1 John 1:1-7	John 14:1-7
M	A.M. 1, 2, 3 P.M. 4, 7	Exod. 14:21-31	1 Pet. 1:1-12	John 14:8-17
T	A.M. 5, 6 P.M. 10, 11	Exod. 15:1-21	1 Pet. 1:13-25	John 14:18-31
W	A.M. 119:1-24 P.M. 12, 13, 14	Exod. 15:22—16:10	1 Pet. 2:1-10	John 15:1-11
T	A.M. 18:1-20 P.M. 18:21-50	Exod. 16:10-22	1 Pet. 2:11-25	John 15:12-27
F	A.M. 16, 17 P.M. 134, 135	Exod. 16:23-36	1 Pet. 3:13—4:6	John 16:1-15
S	A.M. 20, 21:1-7 P.M. 110:1-5, 116, 117	Exod. 17:1-16	1 Pet. 4:7-19	John 16:16-33
Week 3 Easter				
S	A.M. 148, 149, 150 P.M. 114, 115	Exod. 18:1-12	1 John 2:7-17	Mark 16:9-20
M	A.M. 25 P.M. 9, 15	Exod. 18:13-27	1 Pet. 5:1-14	Matt. 3:1-6
T	A.M. 26, 28 P.M. 36, 39	Exod. 19:1-16	Col. 1:1-14	Matt. 3:7-12
W	A.M. 38 P.M. 119:25-48	Exod. 19:16-25	Col. 1:15-23	Matt. 3:13-17
T	A.M. 37:1-18 P.M. 37:19-42	Exod. 20:1-21	Col. 1:24—2:7	Matt. 4:1-11
F	A.M. 105:1-22 P.M. 105:23-45	Exod. 24:1-18	Col. 2:8-23	Matt. 4:12-17
S	A.M. 30, 32 P.M. 42, 43	Exod. 25:1-22	Col. 3:1-17	Matt. 4:18-25
Week 4 Easter				
S	A.M. 63:1-8, 98 P.M. 103	Exod. 28:1-4, 30-38	1 John 2:18-29	Mark 6:30-44
M	A.M. 41, 52 P.M. 44	Exod. 32:1-20	Col. 3:18—4:6	Matt. 5:1-10
T	A.M. 45 P.M. 47, 48	Exod. 32:21-34	1 Thess. 1:1-10	Matt. 5:11-16
W	A.M. 119:49-72 P.M. 49	Exod. 33:1-23	1 Thess. 2:1-12	Matt. 5:17-20
T	A.M. 50 P.M. 114, 115	Exod. 34:1-17	1 Thess. 2:13-20	Matt. 5:21-26
F	A.M. 40, 54 P.M. 51	Exod. 34:18-35	1 Thess. 3:1-13	Matt. 5:27-37
S	A.M. 55 P.M. 138, 139:1-17	Exod. 40:18-38	1 Thess. 4:1-12	Matt. 5:38-48
Week 5 Easter				
S	A.M. 24, 29 P.M. 8, 84	Lev. 8:1-13, 30-36	Heb. 12:1-14	Luke 4:16-30

	Psalm	Old Testament	Epistle	Gospel
M	A.M. 56, 57 P.M. 64, 65	Lev. 16:1-19	1 Thess. 4:13-18	Matt. 6:1-6, 16-18
T	A.M. 61, 62 P.M. 68:1-20, 24-36	Lev. 16:20-34	1 Thess. 5:1-11	Matt. 6:7-15
W	A.M. 72 P.M. 119:73-96	Lev. 19:1-18	1 Thess. 5:12-28	Matt. 6:19-24
T	A.M. 71 P.M. 74	Lev. 19:26-37	2 Thess. 1:1-12	Matt. 6:25-34
F	A.M. 106:1-18 P.M. 106:19-48	Lev. 23:1-22	2 Thess. 2:1-17	Matt. 7:1-12
S	A.M. 75, 76 P.M. 23, 27	Lev. 23:23-44	2 Thess. 3:1-18	Matt. 7:13-21

Week 6 Easter

	Psalm	Old Testament	Epistle	Gospel
S	A.M. 93, 96 P.M. 34	Lev. 25:1-17	James 1:2-8, 16-18	Luke 12:13-21
M	A.M. 80 P.M. 77	Lev. 25:35-55	Col. 1:9-14	Matt. 13:1-16
T	A.M. 78:1-39 P.M. 78:40-72	Lev. 26:1-20	1 Tim. 2:1-6	Matt. 13:18-23
W	A.M. 119:97-120	Lev. 26:27-42	Eph. 1:1-10	Matt. 22:41-46

Eve of Ascension

	A.M. 68:1-20	2 Kings 2:1-15	Rev. 5:1-14	

Ascension Day

	A.M. 8, 47 P.M. 24, 96	Dan. 7:9-14	Heb. 2:5-18	Matt. 28:16-20
F	A.M. 85, 86 P.M. 91, 92	1 Sam. 2:1-10	Eph. 2:1-10	Matt. 7:22-27
S	A.M. 87, 90 P.M. 136	Num. 11:16-17, 24-29	Eph. 2:11-22	Matt. 7:28—8:4

Week 7 Easter

	Psalm	Old Testament	Epistle	Gospel
S	A.M. 66, 67 P.M. 19, 46	Exod. 3:1-12	Heb. 12:18-29	Luke 10:17-24
M	A.M. 89:1-18 P.M. 89:19-52	Josh. 1:1-9	Eph. 3:1-13	Matt. 8:5-17
T	A.M. 97, 99 P.M. 94	1 Sam. 16:1-13	Eph. 3:14-21	Matt. 8:18-27
W	A.M. 101, 109:1-4, 20-30 P.M. 119:121-144	Isa. 4:2-6	Eph. 4:1-16	Matt. 8:28-34
T	A.M. 105:1-22 P.M. 105:23-45	Zech. 4:1-14	Eph. 4:17-32	Matt. 9:1-8
F	A.M. 102 P.M. 107:1-32	Jer. 31:27-34	Eph. 5:1-20	Matt. 9:9-17
S	A.M. 107:33-43, 108:1-6	Ezek. 36:22-27	Eph. 6:10-24	Matt. 9:18-26

Eve of Pentecost

	A.M. 33	Exod. 19:3-8, 16-20	1 Pet. 2:4-10	

The Day of Pentecost

	A.M. 118 P.M. 145	Deut. 16:9-12	Acts 4:18-21, 23-33	John 4:19-26

Psalm	Old Testament	Epistle	Gospel
Eve of Trinity Sunday			
A.M. 104	Exod. 3:1-6	Eph. 3:14-21	
Trinity Sunday			
A.M. 146, 147 P.M. 111, 112, 113	Job 38:1-11, 42:1-5	Rev. 19:4-16	John 1:29-34

The Season After Pentecost

Week 1 (Week of the Sunday Closest to May 11)

	Psalm	Old Testament	Epistle	Gospel
M	A.M. 106:1-18 P.M. 106:19-48	Ezek. 33:1-11	1 John 1:1-10	Matt. 9:27-34
T	A.M. 121, 122, 123 P.M. 124, 125, 126	Ezek. 33:21-33	1 John 2:1-11	Matt. 9:35—10:4
W	A.M. 119:145-176 P.M. 128, 129, 130	Ezek. 34:1-16	1 John 2:12-17	Matt. 10:5-15
T	A.M. 131, 132 P.M. 134, 135	Ezek. 37:21-28	1 John 2:18-29	Matt. 10:16-23
F	A.M. 140, 142 P.M. 141, 143:1-11	Ezek. 39:21-29	1 John 3:1-10	Matt. 10:24-33
S	A.M. 137:1-6, 144 P.M. 104	Ezek. 47:1-12	1 John 3:11-18	Matt. 10:34-42

Week 2 (Week of the Sunday Closest to May 18)

	Psalm	Old Testament	Epistle	Gospel
S	A.M. 42	2 Kings 5:1-15	1 Cor. 9:24-27	Mark 1:40-45
M	A.M. 1, 2, 3 P.M. 4, 7	Prov. 3:11-20	1 John 3:18—4:6	Matt. 11:1-6
T	A.M. 5, 6 P.M. 10, 11	Prov. 4:1-27	1 John 4:7-21	Matt. 11:7-15
W	A.M. 119:1-24 P.M. 12, 13, 14	Prov. 6:1-19	1 John 5:1-12	Matt. 11:16-24
T	A.M. 18:1-20 P.M. 18:21-50	Prov. 7:1-27	1 John 5:13-21	Matt. 11:25-30
F	A.M. 16, 17 P.M. 22	Prov. 8:1-21	2 John 1-13	Matt. 12:1-14
S	A.M. 20, 21:1-7 P.M. 110:1-5, 116, 117	Prov. 8:22-36	3 John 1-15	Matt. 12:15-21

Week 3 (Week of the Sunday Closest to May 25)

	Psalm	Old Testament	Epistle	Gospel
S	A.M. 148, 149, 150 P.M. 114, 115	Prov. 9:1-12	Acts 8:14-25	Luke 10:25-28, 38-42
M	A.M. 25 P.M. 9, 15	Prov. 10:1-12	1 Tim. 1:1-17	Matt. 12:22-32
T	A.M. 26, 28 P.M. 36, 39	Prov. 15:16-33	1 Tim. 1:18—2:8	Matt. 12:33-42
W	A.M. 38 P.M. 119:25-48	Prov. 17:1-20	1 Tim. 3:1-16	Matt. 12:43-50
T	A.M. 37:1-18 P.M. 37:19-42	Prov. 21:30—22:6	1 Tim. 4:1-16	Matt. 13:24-30
F	A.M. 31 P.M. 35	Prov. 23:19-21, 29—24:2	1 Tim. 5:17-22	Matt. 13:31-35

	Psalm	Old Testament	Epistle	Gospel
S	A.M. 30, 32 P.M. 42, 43	Prov. 25:15-28	1 Tim. 6:6-21	Matt. 13:36-43

Week 4 (Week of the Sunday Closest to June 1)

	Psalm	Old Testament	Epistle	Gospel
S	A.M. 63:1-8, 98 P.M. 103	Eccles. 1:1-11	Acts 8:26-40	Luke 11:1-13
M	A.M. 41, 52 P.M. 44	Eccles. 2:1-15	Gal. 1:1-17	Matt. 13:44-52
T	A.M. 45 P.M. 47, 48	Ecles. 2:16-26	Gal. 1:18—2:10	Matt. 13:53-58
W	A.M. 119:49-72 P.M. 49	Eccles. 3:1-15	Gal. 2:11-21	Matt. 14:1-12
T	A.M. 50 P.M. 8, 84	Eccles. 3:16—4:3	Gal. 3:1-14	Mat. 14:13-21
F	A.M. 40, 54 P.M. 51	Eccles. 5:1-7	Gal. 3:15-22	Matt. 14:22-36
S	A.M. 55 P.M. 138, 139:1-17	Eccles. 5:8-20	Gal. 3:23—4:11	Matt. 15:1-20

Week 5 (Week of the Sunday Closest to June 8)

	Psalm	Old Testament	Epistle	Gospel
S	A.M. 24, 29 P.M. 8, 84	Eccles. 6:1-12	Acts 10:9-23	Luke 12:32-40
M	A.M. 56, 57 P.M. 64, 65	Eccles. 7:1-14	Gal. 4:12-20	Matt. 15:21-28
T	A.M. 61, 62 P.M. 68:1-20, 24-36	Eccles. 8:14—9:10	Gal. 4:21-31	Matt. 15:29-39
W	A.M. 72 P.M. 119:73-96	Eccles. 9:11-18	Gal. 5:1-15	Matt. 16:1-12
T	A.M. 71 P.M. 74	Eccles. 11:1-8	Gal. 5:16-24	Matt. 16:13-20
F	A.M. 69:1-23, 31-38 P.M. 73	Eccles. 11:9—12:14	Gal. 5:25—6:10	Matt. 16:21-28
S	A.M. 75, 76 P.M. 23, 27	Num. 3:1-13	Gal. 6:11-18	Matt. 17:1-13

Week 6 (Week of the Sunday Closest to June 15)

	Psalm	Old Testament	Epistle	Gospel
S	A.M. 93, 96 P.M. 34	Num. 6:22-27	Acts 13:1-12	Luke 12:41-48
M	A.M. 80 P.M. 77	Num. 9:15-23, 10:29-36	Rom. 1:1-15	Matt. 17:14-21
T	A.M. 78:1-39 P.M. 78:40-72	Num. 11:1-23	Rom. 1:16-25	Matt. 17:22-27
W	A.M. 119:97-120 P.M. 81, 82	Num. 11:24-33	Rom. 1:28—2:11	Matt. 18:1-9
T	A.M. 34 P.M. 85, 86	Num. 12:1-16	Rom. 2:12-24	Matt. 18:10-20
F	A.M. 88 P.M. 91, 92	Num. 13:1-3, 21-30	Rom. 2:25—3:8	Matt. 18:21-35
S	A.M. 87, 90 P.M. 136	Num. 13:31—14:25	Rom. 3:9-20	Matt. 19:1-12

	Psalm	Old Testament	Epistle	Gospel
Week 7 (Week of the Sunday Closest to June 22)				
S	A.M. 66, 67 P.M. 19, 46	Num. 14:26-45	Acts 15:1-12	Luke 12:49-56
M	A.M. 89:1-18 P.M. 89:19-52	Num. 16:1-19	Rom. 3:21-31	Matt. 19:13-22
T	A.M. 97, 99 P.M. 94	Num. 16:20-35	Rom. 4:1-12	Matt. 19:23-30
W	A.M. 101, 109:1-4, 20-30 P.M. 119:121-144	Num. 16:36-50	Rom. 4:13-25	Matt. 20:1-16
T	A.M. 105:1-22 P.M. 105:23-45	Num. 17:1-11	Rom. 5:1-11	Matt. 20:17-28
F	A.M. 102 P.M. 107:1-32	Num. 20:1-13	Rom. 5:12-21	Matt. 20:29-34
S	A.M. 107:33-43, 108:1-6 P.M. 33	Num. 20:14-29	Rom. 6:1-11	Matt. 21:1-11
Week 8 (Week of Sunday Closest to June 29)				
S	A.M. 118 P.M. 145	Num. 21:4-9, 21-35	Acts 17:22-34	Luke 13:10-17
M	A.M. 106:1-18 P.M. 106:19-48	Num. 22:1-21	Rom. 6:12-23	Matt. 21:12-22
T	A.M. 121, 122, 123 P.M. 124, 125, 126	Num. 22:21-38	Rom. 7:1-12	Matt. 21:23-32
W	A.M. 119:145-176 P.M. 128, 129, 130	Num. 22:41—23:12	Rom. 7:13-25	Matt. 21:33-46
T	A.M. 131, 132 P.M. 134, 135	Num. 23:11-26	Rom. 8:1-11	Matt. 22:1-14
F	A.M. 140, 142 P.M. 141, 143:1-11	Num. 24:1-13	Rom. 8:12-17	Matt. 22:15-22
S	A.M. 137:1-6, 144 P.M. 104	Num. 24:12-25	Rom. 8:18-25	Matt. 22:23-40
Week 9 (Week of the Sunday Closest to July 6)				
S	A.M. 146, 147 P.M. 111, 112, 113	Num. 27:12-23	Acts 19:11-20	Mark 1:14-20
M	A.M. 1, 2, 3 P.M. 4, 7	Num. 32:1-6, 16-27	Rom. 8:26-30	Matt. 23:1-12
T	A.M. 5, 6 P.M. 10, 11	Num. 35:1-3, 9-15, 30-34	Rom. 8:31-39	Matt. 23:13-26
W	A.M. 119:1-24 P.M. 12, 13, 14	Deut. 1:1-18	Rom. 9:1-18	Matt. 23:27-39
T	A.M. 18:1-20 P.M. 18:21-50	Deut. 3:18-28	Rom. 9:19-33	Matt. 24:1-14
F	A.M. 16, 17 P.M. 22	Deut. 31:7-13, 24—32:4	Rom 10:1-13	Matt. 24:15-31
S	A.M. 20, 21:1-7 P.M. 110:1-5, 116, 117	Deut. 34:1-12	Rom. 10:14-21	Matt. 24:32-51
Week 10 (Week of the Sunday Closest to July 13)				
S	A.M. 148, 149, 150 P.M. 114, 115	Josh. 1:1-18	Acts 21:3-15	Mark 1:21-27

	Psalm	Old Testament	Epistle	Gospel
M	A.M. 25 P.M. 9, 15	Josh. 2:1-14	Rom. 11:1-12	Matt. 25:1-13
T	A.M. 26, 28 P.M. 36, 39	Josh. 2:15-24	Rom. 11:13-24	Matt. 25:14-30
W	A.M. 38 P.M. 119:25-48	Josh. 3:1-13	Rom. 11:25-36	Matt. 25:31-46
T	A.M. 37:1-18 P.M. 37:19-42	Josh. 3:14—4:7	Rom. 12:1-8	Matt. 26:1-16
F	A.M. 31 P.M. 35	Josh. 4:19—5:1, 10-15	Rom. 12:9-21	Matt. 26:17-25
S	A.M. 30, 32 P.M. 42, 43	Josh. 6:1-14	Rom. 13:1-7	Matt. 26:26-35

Week 11 (Week of the Sunday Closest to July 20)

	Psalm	Old Testament	Epistle	Gospel
S	A.M. 63:1-8, 98 P.M. 103	Josh. 6:15-27	Acts 22:30—23:11	Mark 2:1-12
M	A.M. 41, 52 P.M. 44	Josh. 7:1-13	Rom. 13:8-14	Matt. 26:36-46
T	A.M. 45 P.M. 47, 48	Josh. 8:1-22	Rom. 14:1-12	Matt. 26:47-56
W	A.M. 119:49-72 P.M. 49	Josh. 8:30-35	Rom. 14:13-23	Matt. 26:57-68
T	A.M. 50 P.M. 66, 67	Josh. 9:3-21	Rom. 15:1-13	Matt. 26:69-75
F	A.M. 40, 54 P.M. 51	Josh. 9:22—10:15	Rom. 15:14-24	Matt. 27:1-10
S	A.M. 55 P.M. 138, 139:1-17	Josh. 23:1-16	Rom. 15:25-33	Matt. 27:11-23

Week 12 (Week of the Sunday Closest to July 27)

	Psalm	Old Testament	Epistle	Gospel
S	A.M. 24, 29 P.M. 8, 84	Josh. 24:1-15	Acts 28:23-31	Mark 2:23-28
M	A.M. 56, 57 P.M. 64, 65	Josh. 24:16-33	Rom. 16:1-16	Matt. 27:24-31
T	A.M. 61, 62 P.M. 68:1-20, 24-36	Judg. 2:1-5, 11-23	Rom. 16:17-27	Matt. 27:32-44
W	A.M. 72 P.M. 119:73-96	Judg. 3:12-30	Acts 1:1-14	Matt. 27:45-54
T	A.M. 71 P.M. 74	Judg. 4:4-23	Acts 1:15-26	Matt. 27:55-66
F	A.M. 69:1-23, 31-38 P.M. 73	Judg. 5:1-18	Acts 2:1-21	Matt. 28:1-10
S	A.M. 75, 76 P.M. 23, 27	Judg. 5:19-31	Acts 2:22-36	Matt. 28:11-20

Week 13 (Week of the Sunday Closest to August 3)

	Psalm	Old Testament	Epistle	Gospel
S	A.M. 93, 96 P.M. 34	Judg. 6:1-24	2 Cor. 9:6-15	Mark 3:20-30
M	A.M. 80 P.M. 77	Judg. 6:25-40	Acts 2:37-47	John 1:1-18
T	A.M. 78:1-39 P.M. 78:40-72	Judg. 7:1-18	Acts 3:1-11	John 1:19-28

	Psalm	Old Testament	Epistle	Gospel
W	A.M. 119:97-120 P.M. 81, 82	Judg. 7:19-8:12	Acts 3:12-26	John 1:29-42
T	A.M. 145 P.M. 85, 86	Judg. 8:22-35	Acts 4:1-12	John 1:43-51
F	A.M. 88 P.M. 91, 92	Judg. 9:1-16, 19-21	Acts 4:13-31	John 2:2-12
S	A.M. 87, 90 P.M. 136	Judg. 9:22-25, 50-57	Acts 4:32—5:11	John 2:13-25

Week 14 (Week of the Sunday Closest to August 10)

	Psalm	Old Testament	Epistle	Gospel
S	A.M. 66, 67 P.M. 19, 46	Judg. 11:1-11, 29-40	2 Cor. 11:21-31	Mark 4:35-41
M	A.M. 89:1-18 P.M. 89:19-52	Judg. 12:1-7	Acts 5:12-26	John 3:1-21
T	A.M. 97, 99 P.M. 94	Judg. 13:1-15	Acts 5:27-42	John 3:22-36
W	A.M. 101, 109:1-4, 20-30 P.M. 119:121-144	Judg. 13:15-24	Acts 6:1-15	John 4:1-26
T	A.M. 105:1-22 P.M. 105:23-45	Judg. 14:1-19	Acts 6:15—7:16	John 4:27-42
F	A.M. 102 P.M. 107:1-32	Judg. 14:20—15:20	Acts 7:17-29	John 4:43-54
S	A.M. 107:33-43, 108:1-6 P.M. 33	Judg. 16:1-14	Acts 7:30-43	John 5:1-18

Week 15 (Week of the Sunday Closest to August 17)

	Psalm	Old Testament	Epistle	Gospel
S	A.M. 118 P.M. 145	Judg. 16:15-31	2 Cor. 13:1-11	Mark 5:25-34
M	A.M. 106:1-18 P.M. 106:19-48	Judg. 17:1-13	Acts 7:44—8:1	John 5:19-29
T	A.M. 121, 122, 123 P.M. 124, 125, 126	Judg. 18:1-15	Acts 8:1-13	John 5:30-47
W	A.M. 119:145-176 P.M. 128, 129, 130	Judg. 18:16-31	Acts 8:14-25	John 6:1-15
T	A.M. 131, 132 P.M. 134, 135	Job 1:1-22	Acts 8:26-40	John 6:16-27
F	A.M. 140, 142 P.M. 141, 143:1-11	Job 2:1-13	Acts 9:1-9	John 6:27-40
S	A.M. 137:1-6 P.M. 144, 104	Job 3:1-26	Acts 9:10-19	John 6:41-51

Week 16 (Week of the Sunday Closest to August 24)

	Psalm	Old Testament	Epistle	Gospel
S	A.M. 146, 147 P.M. 111, 112, 113	Job 4:1-6, 12-21	Rev. 4:1-11	Mark 6:1-6
M	A.M. 1, 2, 3 P.M. 4, 7	Job 4:1, 5:1-11, 17-21, 26-27	Acts 9:19-31	John 6:52-59
T	A.M. 5, 6 P.M. 10, 11	Job 6:1-4, 8-15, 21	Acts 9:32-43	John 6:60-71
W	A.M. 119:1-24 P.M. 12, 13, 14	Job 6:1, 7:1-21	Acts 10:1-16	John 7:1-13
T	A.M. 18:1-20 P.M. 18:21-50	Job 8:1-22	Acts 10:17-33	John 7:14-36

	Psalm	Old Testament	Epistle	Gospel
F	A.M. 16, 17 P.M. 22	Job 9:1-15, 32-35	Acts 10:34-48	John 7:37-52
S	A.M. 20, 21:1-7 P.M. 110:1-5, 116, 117	Job 9:1, 10:1-9, 16-22	Acts 11:1-18	John 8:12-20

Week 17 (Week of the Sunday Closest to August 31)

	Psalm	Old Testament	Epistle	Gospel
S	A.M. 148, 149, 150 P.M. 114, 115	Job 11:1-9, 13-20	Rev. 5:1-14	Matt. 5:1-12
M	A.M. 25 P.M. 9, 15	Job 12:1-6, 13-25	Acts 11:19-30	John 8:21-32
T	A.M. 26, 28 P.M. 36, 39	Job 12:1, 13:3-17, 21-27	Acts 12:1-17	John 8:33-47
W	A.M. 38 P.M. 119:25-48	Job 12:1, 14:1-22	Acts 12:18-25	John 8:47-59
T	A.M. 37:1-18 P.M. 37:19-42	Job 16:16-22, 17:1, 13-16	Acts 13:1-12	John 9:1-17
F	A.M. 31 P.M. 35	Job 19:1-7, 14-27	Acts 13:13-25	John 9:18-41
S	A.M. 30, 32 P.M. 42, 43	Job 22:1-4, 21—23:7	Acts 13:26-43	John 10:1-18

Week 18 (Week of the Sunday Closest to September 7)

	Psalm	Old Testament	Epistle	Gospel
S	A.M. 63:1-8, 98 P.M. 103	Job 25:1-6, 27:1-6	Rev. 14:1-7, 13	Matt. 5:13-20
M	A.M. 41, 52 P.M. 44	Job 32:1-10, 19— 33:1, 19-28	Acts 13:44-52	John 10:19-30
T	A.M. 45 P.M. 47, 48	Job 29:1-20	Acts 14:1-18	John 10:31-42
M	A.M. 119:49-72 P.M. 49	Job 29:1, 30:1-2, 16-31	Acts 14:19-28	John 11:1-16
T	A.M. 50 P.M. 59, 60	Job 29:1, 31:1-23	Acts 15:1-11	John 11:17-29
F	A.M. 40, 54 P.M. 51	Job 29:1, 31:24-40	Acts 15:12-21	John 11:30-44
S	A.M. 55 P.M. 138, 139:1-17	Job 38:1-17	Acts 15:22-35	John 11:45-54

Week 19 (Week of the Sunday Closest to September 14)

	Psalm	Old Testament	Epistle	Gospel
S	A.M. 24, 29 P.M. 8, 84	Job 38:1, 18-41	Rev. 18:1-8	Matt. 5:21-26
M	A.M. 56, 57 P.M. 64, 65	Job 40:1-24	Acts 15:36—16:5	John 11:55—12:8
T	A.M. 61, 62 P.M. 68:1-20, 24-36	Job 40:1, 41:1-11	Acts 16:6-15	John 12:9-19
W	A.M. 72 P.M. 119:73-96	Job 42:1-17	Acts 16:16-24	John 12:20-26
T	A.M. 71 P.M. 74	Job 28:1-28	Acts 16:25-40	John 12:27-36
F	A.M. 69:1-23, 31-38 P.M. 73	Esther 1:1-4, 10-19	Acts 17:1-15	John 12:36-43
S	A.M. 75, 76 P.M. 23, 27	Esther 2:5-8, 15-23	Acts 17:16-34	John 12:44-50

	Psalm	Old Testament	Epistle	Gospel
Week 20 (Week of the Sunday Closest to September 21)				
S	A.M. 93, 96 P.M. 34	Esther 3:1—4:3	James 1:19-27	Matt. 6:1-6, 16-18
M	A.M. 80 P.M. 77	Esther 4:4-17	Acts 18:1-11	Luke 3:1-14
T	A.M. 78:1-39 P.M. 78:40-72	Esther 5:1-14	Acts 18:12-28	Luke 3:15-22
W	A.M. 119:97-120 P.M. 81, 82	Esther 6:1-14	Acts 19:1-10	Luke 4:1-13
T	A.M. 83 P.M. 85, 86	Esther 7:1-10	Acts 19:11-20	Luke 4:14-30
F	A.M. 88 P.M. 91, 92	Esther 8:1-8, 15-17	Acts 19:21-41	Luke 4:31-37
S	A.M. 87, 90 P.M. 136	Hos. 1:1—2:1	Acts 20:1-16	Luke 4:38-44
Week 21 (Week of the Sunday Closest to September 28)				
S	A.M. 66, 67 P.M. 19, 46	Hos. 2:2-14	James 3:1-13	Matt. 13:44-52
M	A.M. 89:1-18 P.M. 89:19-52	Hos. 2:14-23	Acts 20:17-38	Luke 5:1-11
T	A.M. 97, 99 P.M. 94	Hos. 4:1-10	Acts 21:1-14	Luke 5:12-26
W	A.M. 101, 109:1-4, 20-30 P.M. 119:121-144	Hos. 4:11-19	Acts 21:15-26	Luke 5:27-39
T	A.M. 105:1-22 P.M. 105:23-45	Hos. 5:8—6:6	Acts 21:27-36	Luke 6:1-11
F	A.M. 102 P.M. 107:1-32	Hos. 10:1-15	Acts 21:37—22:16	Luke 6:12-26
S	A.M. 107:33-43, 108:1-6 P.M. 33	Hos. 11:1-9	Acts 22:17-29	Luke 6:27-38
Week 22 (Week of the Sunday Closest to October 5)				
S	A.M. 118 P.M. 145	Hos. 13:4-14	1 Cor. 2:6-16	Matt. 14:1-12
M	A.M. 106:1-18 P.M. 106:19-48	Hos. 14:1-9	Acts 22:30—23:11	Luke 6:39-49
T	A.M. 121, 122, 123 P.M. 124, 125, 126	Mic. 1:1-9	Acts 23:12-24	Luke 7:1-17
W	A.M. 119:145-176 P.M. 128, 129, 130	Mic. 2:1-13	Acts 23:23-35	Luke 7:18-35
T	A.M. 131, 132 P.M. 134, 135	Mic. 3:1-8	Acts 24:1-23	Luke 7:36-50
F	A.M. 140, 142 P.M. 141, 143:1-11	Mic. 3:9—4:5	Acts 24:24—25:12	Luke 8:1-15
S	A.M. 137:1-6, 144 P.M. 104	Mic. 5:1-4, 10-15	Acts 25:13-27	Luke 8:16-25
Week 23 (Week of the Sunday Closest to October 12)				
S	A.M. 146, 147 P.M. 111, 112, 113	Mic. 6:1-8	1 Cor. 4:9-16	Matt. 15:21-28

	Psalm	Old Testament	Epistle	Gospel
M	A.M. 1, 2, 3 P.M. 4, 7	Mic. 7:1-7	Acts 26:1-23	Luke 8:26-39
T	A.M. 5, 6 P.M. 10, 11	Jon. 1:1-17	Acts 26:24—27:8	Luke 8:40-56
W	A.M. 119:1-24 P.M. 12, 13, 14	Jon. 1:17—2:10	Acts 27:9-26	Luke 9:1-17
T	A.M. 18:1-20 P.M. 18:21-50	Jon. 3:1—4:11	Acts 27:27-44	Luke 9:18-27
F	A.M. 16, 17 P.M. 22	Amos 5:6-15	Acts 28:1-16	Luke 9:28-36
S	A.M. 20, 21:1-7 P.M. 110:1-5, 116, 117	Amos 6:1-7	Acts 28:17-31	Luke 9:37-50

Week 24 (Week of the Sunday Closest to October 19)

	Psalm	Old Testament	Epistle	Gospel
S	A.M. 148, 149, 150 P.M. 114, 115	Isa. 25:1-9	1 Cor. 10:1-13	Matt. 16:13-20
M	A.M. 25 P.M. 9, 15	Isa. 45:1-7	Rev. 7:1-8	Luke 9:51-62
T	A.M. 26, 28 P.M. 36, 39	Deut. 6:1-9	Rev. 7:9-17	Luke 10:1-16
W	A.M. 38 P.M. 119:25-48	1 Kings 17:8-16	Rev. 8:1-13	Luke 10:17-24
T	A.M. 37:1-18 P.M. 37:19-42	Dan. 12:1-13	Rev. 9:1-12	Luke 10:25-37
F	A.M. 31 P.M. 35	Gen. 2:18-24	Rev. 9:13-21	Luke 10:38-42
S	A.M. 30, 32 P.M. 42, 43	Isa. 53:4-12	Rev. 10:1-11	Luke 11:1-13

Week 25 (Week of the Sunday Closest to October 26)

	Psalm	Old Testament	Epistle	Gospel
S	A.M. 63:1-8, 98 P.M. 103	Jer. 14:7-10, 19-22	1 Cor. 10:15-24	Matt. 18:15-20
M	A.M. 41, 52 P.M. 44	Isa. 1:10-20	Rev. 11:1-14	Luke 11:14-26
T	A.M. 45 P.M. 47, 48	Job 19:23-27	Rev. 11:14-19	Luke 11:27-36
W	A.M. 119:49-72 P.M. 49	Mal. 3:13—4:2-6	Rev. 12:1-6	Luke 11:37-52
T	A.M. 50 P.M. 33	Jer. 23:1-6	Rev. 12:7-17	Luke 11:53—12:12
F	A.M. 40, 54 P.M. 51	Deut. 30:11-14	Rev. 13:1-10	Luke 12:13-31
S	A.M. 55 P.M. 138, 139:1-17	Hab. 2:1-4	Rev. 13:11-18	Luke 12:32-48

Week 26 (Week of the Sunday Closest to November 2)

	Psalm	Old Testament	Epistle	Gospel
S	A.M. 24, 29 P.M. 8, 84	Jer. 26:1-9, 12-15	1 Cor. 12:27—13:13	Matt. 18:21-35
M	A.M. 56, 57 P.M. 64, 65	Exod. 33:18-23	Rev. 14:1-13	Luke 12:49-59
T	A.M. 61, 62 P.M. 68:1-20, 24-36	Jer. 31:15-17	Rev. 14:14—15:8	Luke 13:1-9

	Psalm	Old Testament	Epistle	Gospel
W	A.M. 72 P.M. 119:73-96	Mic. 3:5-12	Rev. 16:1-11	Luke 13:10-17
T	A.M. 71 P.M. 74	Amos 5:18-24	Rev. 16:12-21	Luke 14:18-30
F	A.M. 69:1-23, 31-38 P.M. 73	Zeph. 1:7, 12-18	Rev. 17:1-18	Luke 13:31-35
S	A.M. 75, 76 P.M. 23, 27	Ezek. 34:11-17	Rev. 18:1-14	Luke 14:1-11

Week 27 (Week of the Sunday Closest to November 9)

	Psalm	Old Testament	Epistle	Gospel
S	A.M. 93, 96 P.M. 34	1 Kings 17:8-16	1 Cor. 14:1-12	Matt. 20:1-16
M	A.M. 80 P.M. 77	Joel 1:1-13	Rev. 18:15-24	Luke 14:12-24
T	A.M. 78:1-39 P.M. 78:40-72	Joel 1:15—2:2	Rev. 19:1-10	Luke 14:25-35
W	A.M. 119:97-120 P.M. 81, 82	Joel 2:12-19	Rev. 19:11-21	Luke 15:1-10
T	A.M. 23, 27 P.M. 85, 86	Joel 2:21-27	James 1:1-15	Luke 15:1-2, 11-32
F	A.M. 88 P.M. 91, 92	Joel 2:28—3:8	James 1:16-27	Luke 16:1-9
S	A.M. 87, 90 P.M. 136	Joel 3:9-17	James 2:1-13	Luke 16:10-17

Week 28 (Week of the Sunday Closest to November 16)

	Psalm	Old Testament	Epistle	Gospel
S	A.M. 66, 67 P.M. 19, 46	Hab. 1:1-4, 12—2:1	Phil. 3:13—4:1	Matt. 23:13-24
M	A.M. 89:1-18 P.M. 89:19-52	Hab. 2:1-4, 9-20	James 2:14-26	Luke 16:19-31
T	A.M. 97, 99, 100 P.M. 94	Hab. 3:1-10, 16-18	James 3:1-12	Luke 17:1-10
W	A.M. 101, 109:1-4, 20-30 P.M. 119:121-144	Mal. 1:1, 6-14	James 3:13—4:12	Luke 17:11-19
T	A.M. 105:1-22 P.M. 105:23-45	Mal. 2:1-16	James 4:13—5:6	Luke 17:20-37
F	A.M. 102 P.M. 107:1-32	Mal. 3:1-12	James 5:7-12	Luke 18:1-8
S	A.M. 107:33-43, 108:1-6 P.M. 33	Mal. 3:13—4:6	James 5:13-20	Luke 18:9-14

Week 29 (Week of the Sunday Closest to November 23)

	Psalm	Old Testament	Epistle	Gospel
S	A.M. 118 P.M. 145	Zech. 9:9-16	1 Pet. 3:13-22	Matt. 21:1-13
M	A.M. 106:1-18 P.M. 106:19-48	Zech. 10:1-12	Gal. 6:1-10	Luke 18:15-30
T	A.M. 121, 122, 123 P.M. 124, 125, 126	Zech. 11:4-17	1 Cor. 3:10-23	Luke 18:31-43
W	A.M. 119:145-176 P.M. 128, 129, 130	Zech. 12:1-10	Eph. 1:3-14	Luke 19:1-10
T	A.M. 131, 132 P.M. 134, 135	Zech. 13:1-9	Eph. 1:15-23	Luke 19:11-27

F	A.M. 140, 142 P.M. 141, 143:1-11	Zech. 14:1-11	Rom. 15:7-13	Luke 19:28-40
S	A.M. 137:1-6, 144 P.M. 104	Zech. 14:12-21	Phil. 2:1-11	Luke 19:41-48

Notes

Chapter 1

1. Ben Patterson, *Deepening Your Conversation with God* (Minneapolis: Bethany House Publishers, 2001), 138.
2. C. H. Spurgeon, *The Treasury of David* (Grand Rapids: Zondervan Publishing House, 1976), 3:132
3. Dennis Kinlaw, *This Day with the Master: 365 Daily Meditations* (Grand Rapids: Zondervan Publishing House, 2004), March 8 devotional.
4. Adapted from a message by the late H. Robb French, founder of Florida Evangelistic Association.

Chapter 2

1. Helen E. Bingham, *An Irish Saint* (New York: Evangelical Publishers, 1927), 89.
2. W. E. Vine, *The Divine Inspiration of the Bible* (Brandon, Manitoba: Ritchies' Christian Book Service, 1969), 31.
3. H. Orton Wiley, *The Epistle to the Hebrews*, ed. Morris A. Weigelt (Kansas City: Beacon Hill Press of Kansas City, 1984), 140.
4. Edith Knipmeyer, "Notes from Our Readers," *Women Alive!* September-October 1991, 3.

Chapter 3

1. J. Paterson Smyth, *How to Read the Bible* (New York: James Pott & Co., 1925), 119.
2. Anne Ortlund, *Up with Worship* (Nashville: Broadman & Holman Publishers, 2001), 64.
3. Andrew Murray, *God's Best Secrets* (Grand Rapids: Zondervan Publishing House, 1965), 7.

Chapter 4

1. Andy Stanley, *Visioneering* (Sisters, Oreg.: Multnomah Publishers, 1999), 220.
2. Ronald Rolheiser, *The Holy Longing* (New York: Doubleday, 1999), 74.
3. Jeanne Guyon, *Experiencing the Depths of Jesus Christ* (Sargent, Ga.: The Seed Sowers, 1975), 8.
4. Dallas Willard, *The Divine Conspiracy* (San Francisco: Harper, 1998), 323.
5. Hannah Hurnard, *Hearing Heart* (Wheaton, Ill.: Tyndale House, 1986), 36.
6. Willard, *The Divine Conspiracy*, 356.

Chapter 5

1. Amy Carmichael, *Whispers of His Power* (Old Tappan, N.J.: Fleming H. Revell Co., 1982), 200.

2. Charles Edward White, *The Beauty of Holiness: Phoebe Palmer as Theologian, Revivalist, Feminist, and Humanitarian* (Grand Rapids: Francis Asbury Press of Zondervan Publishing House, 1986), 147.

Chapter 6

1. Susan Annette Muto, *A Practical Guide to Spiritual Reading* (Petersham, Mass.: St. Bede's Publications, 1994), 14.

Chapter 7

1. Bingham, *An Irish Saint*, 93.

Chapter 8

1. E. E. Shelhamer, *Guide to Beginners* (Cincinnati, Ohio: God's Bible School and Revivalist, n.d.), 21.

2. Clarence W. Hall, *Samuel Logan Brengle: Portrait of a Prophet* (Chicago: The Salvation Army Supply and Purchasing Dept. 1933), 184.

3. Jan Winebrenner, *Intimate Faith* (New York: Warner Books, 2003), 136.

Chapter 9

1. Nancy Knight (pseudonym), "Immoral Attraction," *Women Alive!* March-April 1997, 10-11.

Chapter 10

1. Quoted in Michele Novotni and Randy Petersen, *Angry with God* (Colorado Springs: Pinon Press, 2001), 90-91.

2. M. Robert Mulholland Jr., *Shaped by the Word* (Nashville: Upper Room Books, 2000), 138.

Chapter 11

1. Spurgeon, *The Treasury of David*, 3:132.

2. D. L. Moody, *Pleasure and Profit in Bible Study* (Chicago: Moody Press, 1895), 62.

Chapter 12

1. Wesley Duewel, *Mighty Prevailing Prayer* (Grand Rapids: Francis Asbury Press of Zondervan Publishing House, 1990), 290.

2. Dick Eastman, *The University of the Word* (Ventura, Calif.: Regal Books, 1984), 9.

Chapter 13

1. Grade levels listed for these and other versions are available on the Na-

tional Bible Organization's website: <www.nationalbible.org>.

2. G. Campbell Morgan, *The English Bible* (New York: Fleming H. Revell, 1924), 38.

3. Tim LaHaye, *How to Study the Bible for Yourself* (Eugene, Oreg.: Harvest House Publishers, 1998), 42.